The Indigent Rich

THE INDIGENT RICH

**A THEORY OF GENERAL EQUILIBRIUM
IN A KEYNESIAN SYSTEM**

J. W. C. Cumes

PERGAMON PRESS AUSTRALIA

Pergamon Press (Australia) Pty Limited, P.O. Box 544,
  Potts Point, NSW 2011
Pergamon Press Ltd, Headington Hill Hall, Oxford OX3 OBW
Pergamon Press Inc., Fairview Park, Elmsford, NY 10523
Pergamon of Canada Ltd, 207 Queen's Quay West, Toronto 1
Friedr. Vieweg & Sohn, GmbH, Postfach 185, 3300 Braunschweig,
  West Germany

© 1971 J. W. C. Cumes
First published in Australia 1971 by
Pergamon Press (Australia) Pty Limited
Printed in Australia at The Griffin Press, Adelaide
Registered in Australia for transmission by post as a book
National Library of Australia Card Number and SBN 08 017534 1
Library of Congress Catalog Card Number 74 161450

Contents

I
Introduction

It is strange that we can be so wrong about so many things for so long. We seem to be guilty of recurrent economic idiocy. Not just a small idiocy, but idiocy on a grand scale. And it happens about every generation. J. K. Galbraith was probably thinking, *inter alia*, of something like this when he wrote about the error of 'conventional wisdom'. But he has been guilty of the same error himself, along with a multitude of his professional colleagues.

We always think that the same economic problems recur and require the same solutions. History is, in our minds, constantly repeating itself. But, in fact, it isn't. We know full well, from experience, that economic history, despite the old saw, does *not* repeat itself. But we go on acting as though it does.

Consequently, we go on causing ourselves much more trouble —and causing a great many people a great deal more distress —than is necessary. This trouble and distress afflict the domestic economy but their scale is such that they also afflict other economies and, *inter alia*, damage the relationships between the developed countries and the whole of the developing world.

There is a curious similarity between the error into which we have recently fallen and the error into which economists and policy-makers fell in the pre-Keynesian period of the 1930's. Then the theories and policies intensified the very disasters which they were intended to remedy or avert. The same thing is happening now. Not entirely, but in part. Fundamentally, we try to solve our problems of economic disequilibrium by measures which—in practice—intensify them. As in the 1930's, so now we could scarcely do worse if we tried. We act as we do because we think we are still solving economic problems in the context of the 1930's. We are not; but we think so. And the error goes on being repeated however long it would seem to be obvious that the solutions are just as outdated as our conception of the economic environment in which they are being tackled.

To put this a little more specifically, we seek to maintain domestic economic stability by applying or reversing the means which brought us such splendid success at the advent of the Keynesian era. When we are confronted with inflation, we immediately react with policies reversing the fiscal and monetary stimulation which is thought to have caused the inflation. Modern economic policies have created and maintained full employment through active and generally invigorating fiscal and monetary measures. Therefore, the pundits argue that, if these measures go too far and create unacceptable inflation, the solution is to take them off. It is all so simple. Turn on the tap to move the economy up; turn it off to move the economy down.

Almost every economist worth his salt sings or dances to this canticle. Not only do they believe it but they act upon it. And they nod sagely when anyone else—even their political enemies —act upon it.

That it doesn't work is, for them, almost an *obiter dictum*. It *should* work. All the economists agree that it should work. If it seems not to work, then, say the economists, it is because the politicians or the bankers or both have not had the courage or the competence to do the job properly; or the trade unions don't know what is good for them and the country; or the employers don't; or there are 'special factors' which have ruined a good policy in the hands of sincere people.

But the plain fact of the matter is that it does not work. The examples of countries and situations in which it has not worked are now far too many for there to be any doubt that it does not work. The most remarkable examples are Britain, where it has failed to work for more than twenty years; and the United States where it has failed to work ever since that country adopted Keynesian policies round about 1960.

But the persistent refusal to change outworn and obsolete policies—the refusal to abandon 'New Look' fashions in a mini-skirt age—has implications which go far beyond the national economy. This is an age when most countries have entered, are entering or are desperately trying to fit themselves to enter a modern, sophisticated international economic system. Any economic policies adopted by the developed countries—or, in any event, by the major half-dozen or so of the developed countries—are likely to have a lot of impact on a lot of countries. If some of these major developed countries persist with obsolete economic policies, the impact is likely to be disadvantageous for a lot of other countries and could conceivably be disastrous for them. If a couple of these major countries—such as Britain and the United States—are compelled or feel themselves com-pelled simultaneously to press the down button in these policies and to keep their finger on that button for a long period, then a large part of the world economy is going to be a lot worse off than it would otherwise be.

That large part will not necessarily include the other de-veloped countries, or at least will not include them wholly without mitigation. In fact, they will derive some benefit (as well as some loss) from the situation. The countries which will especially suffer will be the developing countries and, to a lesser extent, those countries like Australia and New Zealand which, though developed, are still net importers of capital.

Let us look at this situation a little more closely. Let us look, in particular, at the way in which Keynesian economic policies have affected the relations between the developing and the developed countries in the last twenty years or so.

The literature on the problems of the underdeveloped countries has now grown to massive proportions; and so has the literature on what the developing countries should do, either indepen-dently or in collaboration with others, to find solutions to their problems. But there is comparatively little analysis of how the relations between the developed and the developing countries came to be the way they are; and, where there is such an analysis, it is often conventional, superficial and inaccurate.

Colonialism, imperialism, inhibiting social, economic and political factors all receive some attention; and there can be no doubt that all of these contribute or have contributed to some extent to making the developing countries what they are and to establishing their present relationships with the more sophisticated economies.

Nevertheless, a more fundamental analysis of these latter relationships—an analysis which makes fewer assumptions and which attempts to sketch a rough, theoretical framework—seems to be required. For example, it is sometimes asked why the developing countries do not develop, and the answer is given that it is because they have no capital. It is then asked why do they not get capital from abroad, from those who have it available, and it is answered that the reason is that the risks to capital are too great. This reasoning is plausible but fundamentally invalid. Historically, few things have been quite as venturesome—even reckless—as international capital but it has always tended to go to those places where the profits, relative to risk, are greatest. It is not so much the risks which are a determinant of the flow of international capital as the profits which are hoped, whether wisely or not, to be reaped. Historically, international capital has often turned a blind eye to the risks provided that the profits, however uncertain, would be fat enough if they were realised. The problem in the present phase of relationships between the developed and the developing world is not only that the risks are great in the poor countries, but also that the prospective profits are relatively small, that is, small in relation to the profits offering in the developed countries. Even if the risks were negligible in the developing countries, capital would find a more rewarding home elsewhere.

One overriding reason for this is that the dynamic elements in the world economic situation are, and are most evident, in the developed and not in the developing countries. What the developed countries achieve and their policies—*not* what the developing countries achieve and their policies—are the most significant and, indeed, the dominating factors in the world economic community. What is needed therefore is to examine how the developed world and its policies have evolved to get a clearer idea of what its relations are likely to be, at the most general level, with the developing countries.

This need is especially acute since not simply an evolution, but something like a revolution in economic policy has taken place in the developed countries in the last twenty years. There have been revolutions more violent, but few more complete. The economies of the developed countries are vastly changed not only in their forms, but also in the substance of control and equilibria, from what they were before the Second World War. Given the inevitable dominance of the developed economies, the environment of the whole world economy has therefore changed. This change is not merely one of degree but a change in the essential character in which the world economy operates and its different sectors interact with each other. Some might say it is a change from a bad old world to a brave new world; but, unfortunately, few phases of history, however much improved on earlier phases, are the repository of all the virtues. Some of the vices of the present phase of world economic history seem to apply especially to relationships between the developed and the developing countries. But, in any event, whether these relationships are better or worse than in an earlier period, they are certainly very different. Consequently these relationships must be regarded in a different context from what they were a couple of decades ago; the incentives for a two-way flow of trade and capital—and for certain flows of personnel—must be analysed again in the light of the changed circumstances. But much of the conventional thinking still assumes that these incentives, as well as the context in which they operate, are the same as before. Only the wonder grows that things do not seem to work out as they should.

II
The Keynesian Revolution

Dated from the publication of *The General Theory of Employment, Interest and Money*, the Keynesian revolution is now about thirty-five years old. As revolutions go, it was peaceful and benevolent. The pain it created—and there was some, real or fancied—was vastly compensated by the great, and not wholly material, blessings which it brought. If there had been no Keynes, his revolution would have been achieved by other means; although it might then have been more an evolution than the relatively abrupt transformation which has taken place in economic thinking and economic policy in the past thirty years—or it might have been a more violent revolution which might have swept a lot more things away with it.

Before 1936, practical men, including practical politicians, were already groping towards the economic solutions to which Keynes gave theoretical expression and doctrinal support. Their gropings would probably at length have brought us the policies with which we are familiar today; although, if the process had been too prolonged, the political system in Western countries which Keynes laboured to preserve, might have been shattered beyond hope of recovery. So to those who experienced pain as a result of the Keynesian revolution, perhaps we can fairly say that their pain may eventually have been no less—indeed, it might have been much greater—without the great theoretician, though it may have been drawn out longer and the perpetrator may have been much harder to identify and thus to vilify.[1] They might also draw some solace from the thought that those who believed themselves martyred by his theories were the very ones whom Keynes was anxious to save from a harsher fate. Those to whom his theories brought unmitigated blessings enjoyed those blessings sooner than they would otherwise have done; indeed sooner and more completely than even Keynes himself probably envisaged when his *General Theory* appeared in 1936.

Thirty-five years later few would want to see a Keynesian counter-revolution. Even the most persistent and most bitter opponents are now mostly silenced or no longer heard. The benefits are too monumental. Each active[2] participant in the modern economy has quite suddenly been given the opportunity to enjoy fully, or at least much more fully, the potential of his talents and labours. The Industrial Revolution brought, for most, a distant vision of plenty; the Keynesian revolution gave the vision an imminent reality. If plenty has not been completely realised everywhere yet, it is already no longer a vision in some communities and is a prospect everywhere for this or future generations. The spectre of material want which haunted man through the centuries has, for some communities, disappeared. In these communities, he no longer fears starvation; is not inextricably confined by economic necessity to the monotony of toil or location; and he is no longer bound by his preoccupation with want from realising other ambitions. The waste of man's struggle to reach the moon and stars—if waste it is— is different from the waste of the pyramids and medieval ecclesiastical architecture—if waste those were—in that the struggle can now be encompassed within a superfluity of resources. 'Ein hundesleben ist das wert' has only limited relevance to Cape Kennedy.

But the Keynesian revolution has not been achieved without creating new problems. Perhaps no revolution ever is: it solves

---

[1] He is still vilified in some places, including the United States whose economic and political system perhaps epitomised better than any other the nature of the liberal mood which Keynes wanted to save from destruction under the pressure of massive unemployment and unnecessary economic distress.

[2] The 'inactives'—exposed groups like the old, the ill and the abandoned —still live pretty miserably in most modern economies.

the most biting crisis which called it forth, and, in doing so, justifies itself. It allows man to relax in the aftermath of the agony which prompted his revolt. And, during this period of relative quiescence, he is unaware for a time of the problems— or of the nature of the problems—which are the fruits of his violent reaction to intolerable conditions.

So, with the Keynesian revolution, no one could undo it and few would now want to. But it has created new situations which call for fundamentally new approaches. Some of the consequent problems are only vaguely recognised. At least, the nature of the problems, and especially their origin in the Keynesian revolution, are incompletely understood. 'The shortcomings of economics', wrote J. K. Galbraith, 'are not original error but uncorrected obsolescence.'[3] That generalisation is as misleading as most of its kind, but it does seem true that obsolescence both in our theory and in our conception of the current economic environment have led us to our present incapacity to deal with two major problems deriving from a Keynesian system.

The first of these problems is that of internal economic stability. It has proved to be fairly simple to move a modern economy up to high levels of employment of labour and other resources. It has not proved to be simple to maintain the economy at those levels without introducing internal and external disequilibria which have so far compelled the adoption of policies intended to reduce demand and personal incomes and employment below the highest levels.

The second problem is international. Keynesian policies have, quite unintentionally, created a division between two groups of countries. The membership of these groups of countries cannot be precisely defined at any point of time but they can be broadly identified as the developed and the developing countries. Keynesian policies were fully meaningful only in the particular historical context of those countries, mainly near or bordering the North Atlantic, where the Industrial Revolution originated, and which carried through their economic development quite rapidly, although with cyclical crises of troughs and peaks, during the nineteenth and first half of the twentieth centuries.

[3] J. K. Galbraith, *The Affluent Society*, Houghton Mifflin Co, USA, 1958 (published simultaneously in London by Hamish Hamilton Ltd)

For a long time, the elevation of the peaks rose secularly to higher and higher levels. And then, especially in the 1920's and the 1930's, the peaks were rarely as high as they should have been, the troughs dipped proportionately lower than ever before and were more prolonged, and the need for a new analysis of how the economy worked *in the more advanced countries* became more urgent. The italicised words are vitally important. Like Christianity, liberal democracy, cubism and opera, the Keynesian revolution has had its greatest success where it was a spontaneous response to an evident need; elsewhere its benefits have generally been less apparent. But, more than this, its success in the area in which it originated has, in many of those areas to which it is less relevant, complicated the achievement of economic development similar to that achieved in the North Atlantic countries.

In both the problem of internal economic stability and that of relations between the developed and the developing countries, the evolution of the affluent consumer has played a prominent and, in many ways, a decisive role. It was the Industrial Revolution, and not the Keynesian Revolution, which started this evolution. But it was the Keynesian Revolution which completed it.

III
The Evolution of the Affluent Consumer

Man everywhere began at much the same level of subsistence. Differences arising, for example, from the relative richness of one environment and from relatively greater control of one group over its environment were for centuries—perhaps for millenniums—small in absolute terms, even though they may have been proportionately great at particular times and between particular groups. The Greeks had (in our modern terms) a standard of material living not greatly different from that of the Persians nor much higher than that of their barbarian contemporaries. Roman and Gaul, Carthaginian and Briton, Egyptian and German were, as societies, better or worse endowed in material terms but, in absolute terms of food, clothing, shelter and so on, the differences between the average consumer in each of these societies were not great.

This was still true right up to the time of the Industrial Revolution. The average consumer in India and China probably had less, but not much less, command over economic resources than the average consumer in Europe or North America. To deny all difference between them or to claim that consumption was uniform in all societies would be absurd. Some societies were richer than others; some individuals were so much richer than others that the differences could be immense, although wealth even on the vastest scale could command less than today because the complexity of what the society had to offer was so much less.

The great change began to occur with the Industrial Revolution in Western Europe and North America. But the change transformed the society in some respects quickly, in others, slowly. Among the respects in which the transformation was slow was the increase in living levels of the *average* consumer. In some places, he was perhaps better off in 1850 than in 1750 but the improvement was not great. In some places, even where the Industrial Revolution had been most 'successful', standards of living of the average consumer probably fell between 1750 and 1850 and rose only slowly thereafter. Malthus was by no means blind to the evidence of his own eyes and his own experience.

For a long period after the Industrial Revolution had got under way, therefore, standards of living remained much the same; the average consumer in Asia and Africa had much the same command over resources as the average consumer in Western Europe and North America. Pre-existing differences remained and were gradually reinforced or offset as the Industrial Revolution continued to have an effect which was, however, comparatively slow.

During this period, a market almost anywhere in the world could be quantified almost solely in terms of population. A million Asians constituted just about the same market as a million Europeans or a million Africans. Moreover, at the beginning of the Industrial Revolution, the change was not so much in products as in methods of production. Goods were produced more quickly, in greater quantity and more cheaply, but they remained the same goods intended to meet basic human requirements. Diversification of products, as distinct from sophistication of ways of production, came more slowly and even then was directed only to a small, wealthy section of the population even in the countries most advanced in industrial development. A wealthy section existed in most communities, whether in Europe, North America, Asia or Africa, though the sources of wealth and the identity of the wealthy were undergoing change in the industrialising countries.

A situation existed, therefore, which contained three main elements. First, a rapidly increasing productive capacity in the industrialising countries. Second, a static or only slowly rising level of living of the average consumer in the industrialising countries. And, third, an increasing or prospectively increasing, but still relatively small, difference between living levels of the average consumer in the countries which were industrialising and those which were not. (Not all of the new wealth accrued all of the time to the industrialising countries. Some primary-producing countries like Australia made great, though erratic, advances during the nineteenth century in gross production and in income per head of population, even though industrialisation was small or negligible.)

There was a tendency for supply to respond to capacity rather than demand, and then to seek out demand to absorb it. In the circumstances outlined above, a market in the non-industrialising countries was as good or nearly as good as at home. With their greater command over resources, the industrialising countries had the power, or quickly came to have the power, to annex territory or to establish spheres of commercial influence. Where this was not possible or desirable, they negotiated for markets in sovereign, non-industrialising countries.

Commercially, the countries which were annexed, or brought within spheres of influence, or even merely negotiated with, were important to the industrialising countries. Without them, the industrialising countries would have been less able to maintain their growth, to expand their capital resources and, even though gradually, to raise the level of living of their own average consumer. Without them, the evolution of the affluent consumer in the developed countries would have been a good deal slower.

This is not to say that the industrialising countries necessarily engaged in 'exploitation' of the others. It might have been possible, if slower, for each industrialising country to carry through its own development on the basis of its own market. This would have left the non-industrialising countries as completely outside the changes in market production as, let us say, Tibet or Burundi. While it might have given some assurance against or helped to safeguard the industrialising countries from charges of 'exploitation', it would have delayed bringing the developing countries into a process the rewards of which have, in recent years, become their most urgent and most absorbing preoccupation. (Some of the developing countries which were never colonies seem sometimes almost to regret their failure to achieve colonial status during the nineteenth and earlier twentieth centuries.)

As well as being a market, the non-industrialising countries were also a source of food and raw materials. If levels of living in the industrialising countries did not rise rapidly, population did; and agricultural and raw materials production could not always keep pace either with population increase or with the increased demands of an expanding industrial production. The non-industrialising countries were therefore needed as supply sources and, where they could negotiate and needed to negotiate to supply food and raw materials, their negotiating position was strengthened because of their importance as a market to the industrialising countries. Until the producer—the worker as well as the employer—in the industrialising countries would be affluent enough to be able to buy most of his own product, outlets would be needed for surplus production in the non-industrialising markets. These latter markets would be needed—and could be vitally important—for a longer or shorter period, depending on whether the evolution to mass affluence would be quick or slow in the industrialising countries, both as a whole and separately.

In retrospect, there was a peculiar harmony and seeming rightness about this situation. Everything seemingly fitted nicely into place. Everything was for the best in the best of all possible commercial worlds. The non-industrialising countries were 'needed'; they could, in some measure, look the industrialising countries in the face in the contribution they made to the productive and market situation; and, around a negotiating table, the sovereign non-industrialising countries at least could hope to strike a bargain with their more advanced fellows because they had something valuable and even vital to offer as well as ask.

But, even in retrospect, the world was far from perfect. The harmony between industrialising countries and others did not necessarily break down; although sometimes that happened too. But, more importantly, balance within the industrialising countries themselves was often upset. Equilibrium at the highest possible level of economic activity was an abnormal situation; and when boom lapsed or plunged into depression, the non-industrialising countries suffered too. Although, during the nineteenth century cyclical depressions were not always deep and lasting, they came fairly frequently and they were always painful for many people. The boom conditions in the early Australian colonies in the 1830's suddenly changed into an acute depression. 'With the beginning of the forties', said one commentator, 'there came a sharp fall in the British prices for wool, and the prosperity which the pastoral industry had enjoyed throughout the thirties suffered an eclipse.'[1] The causes of the slump were more complex than this suggests; but true it was that, in 1841 and subsequent years, land and flocks lost most of their value and it became more economic to boil a sheep down for its fat than keep it to sell its wool. 'Sheep had brought 35s. a head in 1839: in 1843 they were sold at "sixpence a head and the station given in". Horses worth "£50 to £70 for the commonest hack" in 1839 went for £7 in 1843. Fat cattle went at 50s. as compared with £10 to £12.'[2] Later in the century, the boom of the 1880's gave way to the deep depression of the 1890's, when 'British investors looked askance at Australian public and private securities',[3] the value of wool was low, and persistent drought hit the pastoral industry of New South Wales. A decade in which Australians had achieved a standard of living probably comparable to that anywhere else in the world and in which (1882-91) almost a million people migrated to Australia, increasing its population by 41 per cent, was followed by a period of bank collapses and unemployment, in which there was a net emigration from Australia in ten of the fifteen years from 1892 to 1906, a net loss of 24,000 by emigration.

Apart from the economic winds which blew hot and cold for the non-industrialising countries and which brought these cyclical economic disasters, there were political effects too. The nineteenth century was the epic period of colonialism and the stimulus provided by industrialisation—though not the only cause—was almost certainly a major, if not the major spur to colonialism. Countries and peoples throughout the non-European world lost their independence—although sometimes they had little more than a village-type political organisation anyway—and had their

[1] H. Burton, in *The Peopling of Australia*, Melbourne University Press, 1928
[2] Edward Shann, *An Economic History of Australia*, Cambridge University Press, 1930, p. 106
[3] ibid., p. 349

social and cultural inheritance destroyed or damaged or put at risk.

All this must be acknowledged. The world right up to 1945 was, in its long-term character, an economically dynamic but also terrifyingly unstable world. The anarchy of the free market, especially as it manifested itself in the 1930's, had to be controlled. Although the imperatives to end European domination were of a lesser order, this domination was essentially temporary, and related to a particular phase of economic history. At the end of the Second World War, it stood to be corrected, along with the control of the free market. Indeed, the two things went together: control of the former anarchy of the free market would bring with it an end of the stimulus to colonialism. The direct connection between the two was not seen in 1945 and has not been seen ever since with the clarity it deserves. But it was there nevertheless.

And it was in this fact that the harmony between different parts of the world economy in the pre-Keynesian era resided. Despite the constantly recurring disequilibria, the industrialising (or developed) countries were important to the non-industrialising (or developing) countries and—most significantly—the reverse was also true. Indeed, it was because of the constantly recurring disequilibria, that the developing (including the colonial) countries were so important to the developed countries. When boom lapsed or plunged into depression, even marginal markets took on a great importance. The threat, quite apart from the actuality, of supply outrunning demand gave an importance to small and perhaps distant markets which would never have been the case if equilibrium—equilibrium at full capacity levels of supply—had been a constant condition.

So markets everywhere, inside and outside the industrialising countries, were significant to those countries which were caught up in and carried through the Industrial Revolution. The non-industrial countries were to be wooed, won and held. In some cases, they were conquered and colonised. In others they were won, for a period, by negotiation of a trade or other agreement. In all cases, they were, or were thought to be, worth the effort or sacrifice whether this was expressed in terms of military and administrative costs and responsibilities or in terms of granting reciprocal access, after negotiation, to the products of some or all of the non-industrialised countries.

In many ways—although they could hardly have known it—this was the great period of the non-industrialised countries and territories. They were needed by the newly emerged industrial countries; without them, growth would have been less rapid and even less stable than it was. Their role, if not indispensable to the whole process, made that process more dynamic, more exciting and less painful than it would otherwise have been.

But that situation—like any other economic situation—was a phase in a process, not an unalterable conclusion. It was not to last.

By the time of the Second World War, individual incomes and consequently living standards in the developed countries had made considerable advances. The average consumer in all of these countries was still far from affluent and the Great Depression of the 1930's had just clearly underlined that his income and living standards were far from assured. The great change came only after the Second World War with the advent of Keynesian policies. The essence of these policies was that full employment should be achieved and maintained by stimulation of demand both for consumption and investment. As an integral element in these policies, governments constructed intricate regimes of social welfare, installed built-in stabilisers and fortified or inaugurated other devices intended to sustain personal income and demand. In so doing, governments inaugurated stable—and growing—demand and they also virtually guaranteed stable—and dynamic—consumption. This sort of demand and consumption could not be realised and maintained by an affluent few; it had to come—could only come—from an affluence—never known in any society before—running right through the economy. Whether the affluent consumer was an end-product or a by-product is of little consequence; certainly he was an inevitable result of Keynesian policies. He—and the conditions with the potential to produce him—had been evolving for two hundred years, since the beginning of the Industrial Revolution. In the end, he emerged suddenly. When he did, he—the affluent consumer—changed, in one way or another, the whole world.

The changes which the affluent consumer brought about

demanded—if we were not to be guilty of uncorrected obsolescence—a new analysis of a fundamentally new economic situation. That new situation emerged suddenly by the standards of most political, economic or social change; but it was nevertheless a change which carried, superficially at least, some of the characteristics of the earlier period into the new situation. Indeed, perhaps it is always true that elements which were highly significant in a prior situation seldom disappear completely in the new situation which succeeds it. But their decline in consequence may be of such an order that they lose any decisive quality and no longer have any marked effect on world economic relationships. Just when the markets of the non-industrialised countries ceased to have decisive significance for the developed countries cannot be fixed with precision; but the trend towards this new situation was associated with the emergence of the affluent consumer. It began in the later thirties and became increasingly evident in the years after the Second World War. The denouement to the trend came with the age of affluence.

IV
The Age of Affluence

The change in the world economy attributable to the affluent consumer was constructed from three main elements. First, the rise in the level of living of the average consumer in the advanced countries—a rise which is continuing and, at least in some advanced countries, accelerating. Second, the achievement of steady (though for the most part, rapid) economic growth at high levels of human and capital employment and without the occurrence of anything like the economic depressions which the advanced economies suffered before 1939. Third, the ever-increasing sophistication of industrial production which is both a reflection of and a stimulus to the constantly more sophisticated consumer in the advanced countries.

What this has meant is that the average consumer in the advanced countries has so much greater command over resources than his 'counterpart' in the developing countries that the two are no longer comparable economic phenomena. It also means that the average consumer in the advanced countries exercises a *constantly* high and increasing demand; recessions are largely government-induced for reasons of restoring external or internal balance in an over-dynamic growth situation; and, this being so, the need to hedge against domestic instability by securing marginal, overseas markets has been greatly reduced. Finally, it means that many of the products—the more sophisticated products—of the industry of the advanced countries can find a market of scale only within their own domestic economies and those of their advanced fellows. The differences between the level of living of the average consumer in the advanced and the developing countries is reflected partly in differences in the amounts consumed of certain items (the German consumes more food than the Indian), but also in variations in the type of product consumed (the average German drives a Volkswagen, an Opel, or a Mercedes; the average Indian walks or rides a bicycle—or stays at home).

With the maturing of economies, there is, apart from quantitative and qualitative changes in commodity demand by consumers, a change in the proportion of demand directed to services. In a subsistence economy and in an economy in the early stages of the industrialising process, the demand for services is a relatively small proportion of aggregate demand. As the economy matures, more than half the economy's gross product and perhaps substantially more than half the economy's labour force will be engaged in the provision of services. This causes a concentration of population in large towns, cities and, ultimately, in extensive metropolitan areas, or megalopolises, covering a large, continuous built-up region. The gold-rush effect of service industries will be discussed elsewhere. Here, the point to be made is that the development of service industries means necessarily a turning inwards of the economy rather than the looking outwards which was symptomatic of the earlier stages of the industrialisation process. There is, of course, some export and import of services, especially in banking and finance, including insurance, commercial services and in the tourist industry. But, generally, the development of service industries means that the economy tends to be proportionately less interested in outside markets and outside supply sources. Within this general trend, where services are supplied to or received from points outside the domestic economy, the strong tendency will be for this exchange to be with other mature economies. Exchange of services with developing countries (except in the sense of use of labour which will be discussed later) is relatively insignificant.

However, for the moment, we can leave aside this complication of the development of the service industries. What we want to do now is to try to establish the quantitative importance and growth of the markets of the developing countries as compared with those of the developed countries. This can be illustrated, in macroeconomic terms, by examining some statistics of national and per capita incomes.

According to the United Nations Statistical Office, per capita income in India in 1955 was £stg.19. By 1962 it had risen to £stg.25. Per capita income in West Germany was £stg.224 in 1955 and £stg.426 in 1962. Although the proportionate increase in income in India—almost one-third—was large, the absolute increase of £stg.6 per capita (less than £stg.1 per year) was small. By contrast, both the proportionate and the absolute increase in per capita income in Germany was enormous. It almost doubled in seven years and the absolute increase was £stg.202 (£stg.29 per year). Between 1955 and 1962, the per capita income of each German *increased* by about eight times the per capita income achieved by each Indian at the end of the period. In other words, if the population of West Germany was 55 million and the population of India was 450 million, the *increase* in German income over the seven-year period (55 million x £stg.202 = £11,110 million) was almost equal to the *total* income of India at the end of the period (450 million x £stg.25 = £11,250 million).

Between 1962 and 1968, the changes were even more dramatic. Per capita income in India increased from £stg.25 to just under £stg.30 in the six-year period—that is, at less than £stg.1 a year, much the same as in the earlier seven-year period. By 1968, per capita income in West Germany had increased from £stg.426 to £stg.706 over the six-year period—that is, an average annual increase of nearly £stg.47 per capita, more than half as much again as the annual increase in the earlier seven-year period. The fifty-eight million Germans at the end of the period had *added* more, £stg.16,240 million, to their income than the total national income of £stg.15,900 million of the 530 million Indians at the end of the period. In the age of affluence which the German experience identifies, therefore, the absolute size of the national income of developed countries, the rate of growth of their national incomes, and the per capita income of their average consumer, are so large that a market equal to the national income even of the largest developing country can be added every year or every few years to an advanced economy, depending on the size of the developed country; and the average consumer in some developed countries can add as much in about a week to his income as the average consumer in a developing country might add in a year.

When it comes to the United States, the contrasts are even more startling. The United States can, and in the recent past often has, *added* to its gross national product in a matter of months an amount equal to the whole gross national product of a country as large as India. In the 1950's and early 1960's, when the percentage growth in per capita income was relatively low, United States per capita income increased by £stg.153 over the seven-year period from 1955 to 1962 (about £stg.22 a year). During this period, if the United States population is taken as 200 million, the economy *added* to its income every two and a half years an amount almost equal to the total income of the 450 million Indians. Over the seven-year period, additional income (and therefore markets) had been added to the United States economy nearly three times as great as the whole income (and markets) of India. Even if United States producers nourished the impossible hope of supplying the whole of the Indian market, they would be struggling for a total market only one-third as large as the seven-year growth in the market right at their own factory gates.

The growth in the United States economy since 1962 has been even more dramatic, both in gross and per capita terms. By the late 1960's, the United States was adding to its gross national product the equivalent of the Indian economy every eight or nine months. And the sensational growth of the Japanese economy, already under way in the 1950's, miraculously continued at a rate which can fairly be regarded as fantastic by any standards of the past. The reasonable prospects are that the growth of the United States and the Japanese economies will continue at much their same average rate over a period of years in the future. This will be so even if the hesitations in growth brought about by the attempts of governments to cool down 'overheated' economies, continue in the future. Even in this event, both economies will increase massively, with a marked tendency of the Japanese economy steadily and fairly rapidly to overhaul the United States economy (and, long before that, incidentally, to overhaul the

Soviet economy). If policies can be found which will enable these periodic hesitations to be avoided, the increases will be even greater.

In either event, the United States and Japanese economies will, during the seventies and eighties, add to their national incomes each year—certainly each year on average—amounts equal to the combined national incomes of whole groups of the largest developing countries. Though to a lesser degree, the same type of experience will be shared by the other developed countries. For all the developed countries, the present age of affluence at the beginning of the 1970's will, by the 1980's, seem like an age of spartan living if the prospective improvements in per capita income are realised. This will be so whether we assess these prospective improvements in the context of periodic hesitations in the economy, or whether we calculate that these hesitations will be eliminated. All of these countries will add each year a huge new domestic market to their existing domestic market and will be confronted with—presented with or tempted with might be better terms—vast new markets in the economies of their fellow developed countries.

Apart from size, we need to think about the stability of markets. No markets are completely stable, completely reliable. In the developed countries, they are less stable and reliable than they might be because of the current theory and practice for restoring stability when the economy becomes seemingly overextended. If that theory and practice can be improved, the stability and reliability of the developed economies will be greatly enhanced. But, even now, in terms of stability, either there is not much to choose between the advanced countries and some of the developing countries *at their best* or the choice lies very clearly with the advanced countries. This is particularly so for export and import markets. Violent fluctuations in prices of primary commodities and forced-draught economic development in the developing countries have meant that the purchases of many developing countries may be greatly expanded and then drastically curtailed almost from one year to the next. If producers in advanced countries are seeking steady, reliable, expanding markets, then they must no longer think of seeking compensation in developing countries' markets for fluctuations in their own domestic markets, but rather of the disruption which too great attention to—and too great temporary success in—markets in developing countries could cause to their own stable growth, otherwise fairly well assured by a strong and expanding home market.

But that is not all. Leaving service industries aside, the dynamism of the modern industrial economy is not based, as it was in the past, on textiles, soap and beer. It is based on a variety of sophisticated consumer goods—such as motor vehicles, domestic appliances and a wide variety of gadgetry and personal luxury—which is far beyond the purchasing power of the consumer with a per capita income of £25 or £50 or £100 a year. It is not simply that these consumers will buy *less* of these things than their wealthier counterparts in the advanced countries. Except for that relatively small and probably fairly constant group at the top of the income ladder, they will buy *none*, because they cannot. There is and no doubt will continue to be a market for, say, motor cars in Asian and African countries but generally it will be small relative to that in the developed countries and not likely to make the difference between dynamism and depression in the major producing countries. Consequently, it is not likely, for example, to be something for which governments of developed countries will bargin seriously in trade and tariff negotiations.

We have been dealing with consumer goods, including consumer durables. But what about capital goods? Perhaps a case can be made out that the developing countries do and will provide a substantial market for the output of the capital-goods industries of the advanced economies. Perhaps these developing markets could be decisive in maintaining these capital-goods industries at full production.

First of all, a word about the sophistication of the needs of newly industrialising countries. By and large, these countries first establish simple processing industries for food, drink, textiles and raw materials (smelting or primary refining of tin, copper and other materials). Generally, the capital equipment for these industries is produced by the advanced countries but, as they have gone on to more advanced manufacturing stages, this equipment has formed a smaller and smaller part of their capital-goods production. Some countries will want steel mills; some will want atomic reactors. This will reflect the different stages of development and the varying ambitions of the various developing countries, which do not form one homogeneous group. They come in all the colours and shades of the development spectrum; and we classify them all under the heading of 'developing countries' only to simplify the argument towards a general theory.

But while this diversity must be acknowledged, the countries right across the developing spectrum will require less sophisticated—perhaps more labour-intensive—capital equipment than the developed countries.

Second, they will also want—or be able to acquire—much less of it. Certainly, the developing countries are anxious to develop their economies as quickly as possible. Their principal preoccupation in recent years has seemed to be their gross national product and their per capita income, and the means by which these two gods may be appeased. All of them have three-, five-, ten-, or umpteen-year development plans. Some of them make a strenuous effort to fulfil them. All of them complain if the plans are not fulfilled and blame—usually—the wealthier countries for not sufficiently meeting the capital and technical needs of their poorer brethren.

If it is true that not to have a development plan is to be naked among one's well-dressed fellows, so it is true too that these development plans look to capital rather than consumption expenditure and thus to the import of a wide range of capital goods. Doesn't it therefore follow that these development plans of the poorer countries provide a market for the capital-goods production of the developed countries?

To some extent, of course, they will. In aggregate, the demand of the poorer countries for capital goods will be large, as indicated by the table for gross investment given on page 26. Not *all* of these expenditures will be on capital goods imported from abroad but a sufficient proportion will be, to amount to a considerable aggregate demand.

But the demand of the developing countries must be kept in perspective. The total investment of a huge developing country like India under one of its five-year plans is no more than the investment made in one of the major cities in the advanced countries—like New York or London or Tokyo—in a matter of a few months. Billions of dollars are invested almost unnoticed every month in these major cities while some of the largest of the developing countries agonise over the investment of a fraction of this amount to try to get their economies moving forward more rapidly—or even moving forward at all. (The demand in the developing countries for individual capital items will be more a windfall—a bonus—to individual firms in the advanced countries than staple income. The supply of equipment for a tin smelter or a steel mill; the construction of a dam or a road or a bridge; or the supply of equipment for a mine can be of great value to an individual manufacturing or construction firm; but few can build their future on such windfall gains.)

Investment in the poorer countries is small not only compared with investment in the giant economies like the United States and the Soviet Union and Japan; but even in relation to quite small members of the advanced community like Australia or Belgium or Sweden. Before the outbreak of the civil war in 1966, Nigeria—the most populous and one of the richest countries in the whole of Africa—contemplated capital expenditure of about $US2000 million over the whole six-year period of her then current economic development plan. This compared with *annual* gross fixed capital expenditure in 1965-66 in a relatively small developed economy like Australia of $US6233 million. Now that the war has ended, Nigeria—assisted by large and rapidly increasing oil revenue—contemplates development expenditure of about $US1250 million a year—about four times the annual expenditure contemplated in 1966. Even if this rate is achieved, it will compare with investment in Australia now running at the rate of about $US8700 million a year and increasing at an annual rate of about $US700 million. Although the planned development expenditure by Nigeria is now a greater proportion of actual Australian investment, the absolute difference between the two in 1966 was about $US6000 million; now it has risen to about $US7500 million. In brief, even though their development expenditure gets bigger, the relative significance of the developing countries as points of investment interest tends constantly to grow less.

To illustrate this point with more precision statistically, the following table shows, in round figures, the total investment of some selected developing countries in Africa, Asia and Latin America:

GROSS DOMESTIC CAPITAL FORMATION
DEVELOPING COUNTRIES
1967 or 1968

	$US (million)	Population (million)
Ghana	230	8.5
Tanzania	150*	12.5
Kenya	255	10.5
United Arab Republic (Egypt)	787*	32.5
Indonesia	2,135	117.0
Pakistan	1,952*	111.5
Thailand	1,290*	34.5
Argentina	3,570	23.5
Brazil	2,800*	90.5

* 1967

Source: Derived from *United Nations Yearbook of National Accounts Statistics*, 1969: and *Demographic Yearbook*, 1969

The gross capital formation of these nine countries, with a population of hundreds of millions of people, totals just over $US13 billion. The gross capital formation in Australia, with a population of about twelve million was, at about the same time, about $US8 billion.

To give this a larger perspective, the following table sets out, in round figures, the aggregate annual investment, public and private, in some of the developed countries both large and small:

GROSS DOMESTIC CAPITAL FORMATION
DEVELOPED COUNTRIES
1968

	$US (million)	Population (million)
Sweden	4,130	7.8
Belgium	4,460	9.6
France	29,000	50.0
Germany	32,875	58.5
Japan	50,146	102.0
United States	154,700	203.0

Source: Derived from *United Nations Yearbook of National Accounts Statistics*, 1969: and *Demographic Yearbook*, 1969

The smallest of these countries, Sweden, with a population of 7.8 million, has gross capital formation considerably larger than any of the developing countries listed. The country with a roughly equivalent population, Ghana—population 8.5 million—has gross capital formation only 5 per cent as large or about half the increase in gross capital formation usually achieved in Sweden each year.

Development expenditures in the poorer countries are therefore small compared with those in the advanced countries. But that is not the whole of the story. There are three associated points to be made. These relate to:

1 The amounts of development expenditure which are met from the labour and other resources of the developing countries themselves, that is, those amounts which are not spent on imports;

2 The need, or otherwise, for capital-goods producers in developed countries to find markets in developing countries; and, most importantly,

3 The capacity of developed countries to provide capital goods to developing countries, and the extent to which and the terms on which they should do so.

As the preceding tables show, gross investment in the developing countries is only a small proportion of gross investment in the developed countries; indeed, this is, in effect, a basic function and characteristic of development. But, apart from gross investment being relatively small, most of the investment will have to be made from local resources. Most of it will use local labour— for the building of roads, the construction of factories, and so on —and as much finance as possible will have to be mobilised locally, mainly by the government, if private institutions have not matured sufficiently. 'Developing countries . . . will . . . continue to adopt vigorous measures for a fuller mobilisation of the whole range of their domestic financial resources and for ensuring the most effective use of available resources, both internal and external. For this purpose, they will pursue sound fiscal and monetary policies and, as required, remove institutional obstacles through the adoption of appropriate legislative and administrative reforms. . . . Every effort will be made to mobilise private savings through financial institutions, thrift societies, post office savings banks and other saving schemes, and through expansion of opportunities for saving for specific purposes such as education and housing. The available supply of saving will be channelled to investment projects in accordance with their development priorities.'[1] There is no alternative to this. Developing countries do not have the reserves or a sufficient surplus on current earnings wholly to finance their development from overseas—even if it made economic sense to do so.

In quantitative terms, the import market for capital goods in the developing countries will therefore be much smaller than the gross capital formation figures indicate. It will be tiny compared with gross capital formation in the developed countries; and it will remain that way. At least, it will remain that way for a long time ahead; let us say until the end of the century. The developed countries' demand for capital goods ten years from now will be massive compared with what it is today. The demand of the United States alone in 1980 will dwarf anything we have known in any collection of countries or indeed in the whole of the world economy at any previous time in recorded history. No seriously imaginable growth in demand for capital goods in the developing countries can conceivably rival—or have much effect on—the virtually certain growth in demand for capital goods in the developed countries themselves.

This leads to our second point which is the need or otherwise for capital-goods producers in developed countries to find markets for their products in the developing countries. In most conceivable circumstances, this need just does not exist. Domestic demand and demand in fellow developed countries is virtually certain to be so large—and so stable and assured—that producers in developed countries will be almost wholly preoccupied with satisfying this demand. There will be individual firms which—as we have already observed—will make sales to developing countries. For these firms, there is and will continue to be benefit.

But, nationally, there is not. Nationally, the impact of sales will be of quite a different order. The attempt to meet any substantial demand in the developing countries in addition to

[1] *An International Development Strategy for the Second United Nations Development Decade*, adopted by the 25th session of the United Nations General Assembly in 1970, para. 41

domestic demand could lead to disequilibrium in the domestic economy. Instead of being of benefit to the national economy, supply of capital goods in substantial quantities to the developing countries could lead to domestic inflation and strain on the external balance of payments.

We must keep clearly in mind that, under modern economic policies, the advanced economies will be operating continuously at a high level of employment of labour and other economic resources and a high level of consumption. It will, at any time, be operating at a level below full stretch only by a margin which is politically acceptable—a margin which is tending constantly to shrink. Any transfer of production out of the economy must be related to this high employment, high consumption and high social-welfare situation.

At full employment of labour and capital, the demands of consumption and investment should ideally be exactly equal to the supply of consumer and capital goods. If the supply of either is reduced for some reason, that reduction will, in itself, have a destabilising effect. If capital goods are supplied to another developed country, this is likely to be part of a reciprocal supply process. Reciprocity might depend on a bilateral or a more complex multilateral relationship. But the pattern is likely to be constant or constantly recurring; and it is likely, with some shortcomings here and there, to maintain a balance between supply and demand in the economy. In any event, there is nothing in the supply relationship among developed countries which is inherently or necessarily destabilising.

But the supply relationship for capital goods between a developed and a developing country is fundamentally different. That relationship is essentially destabilising. It is inherently and necessarily destabilising—although the effect may be less in some circumstances than in others, and may sometimes be offset by other quite unrelated factors such as fortuitous and temporary inflow of capital from another developed country.

This leads us to consideration of the third of those questions which were adumbrated above; and it is perhaps the most important of those questions. It is this: if an advanced country produces the necessary capital goods, can it and should it provide them to the developing countries? If so, to what extent should it provide them and—the most vital question of all—on what terms, cash, loan or gift should they be provided?

The answer to the first part of the question is fairly clear. We operate in an exchange—not a subsistence—economy and it is an *international* exchange economy. Sometimes, we are under a temptation to proclaim loudly that our economic system is *increasingly* an international exchange system. The temptation should be resisted. Or at least it should be examined properly and then proclaimed only if, and to the extent that, it accords with the facts. The more a country becomes integrated in a group of highly developed countries, the more important relatively as well as absolutely will international exchange become. But, on the other hand, the more that modern economies become service economies—that is, the greater the resources devoted to tertiary industries providing, for the most part, services direct from one individual to another—the less relatively will they be involved in international exchange.

However, to the extent that modern economies—and certainly highly developed economies—operate in an exchange system and in an *international* exchange system, it seems to follow that they should supply capital goods to developing countries if they have these goods available for sale. (We are here ignoring any political and strategic factors and considering only the reasonably free play of market forces.) In theory, Belgium should be no less willing to supply capital goods to Gabon than to Germany, to Laos than to Luxembourg.

But to what extent should she do so? Again, the answer is, in theory, to whatever extent it has capital goods available and the developing countries can exert an effective demand for them. Here we come to the crucial part of the question: what is the nature of the effective demand which the developing countries can exert and, derived from that, what are the terms on which developed countries should supply them with capital goods?

If developing countries buy capital goods for cash, they become normal exports of the developed countries and the resources earned from sales are immediately available for purchases to satisfy demand on the home market. Except perhaps momentarily, no disequilibrium between supply and demand is thus introduced into the home market because of the export of these capital goods for cash. Indeed, it may be that the supply position is improved because—at least in theory—the exporting developed country has exchanged goods which she was more efficient in producing for goods which she would have produced less efficiently, that is, with a greater outlay of her labour and other economic resources.

If developing countries buy capital goods on credit, the impact on the developed economy will depend on the terms of the credit. Immediately, the developed country will obtain no requital of resources which will enable it to offset any supply-demand disequilibrium resulting from transfer of the credit-exports to the developing market. If its international reserves are sufficient or, for example, if the credit to the developing countries is offset by buoyant current earnings or by an inflow of capital from other sources, then the unrequited credit-exports can be compensated and none of the symptoms of disequilibrium need result. If these compensating factors are not present, then a deterioration in the balance of payments and international reserves might disclose such an external disequilibrium that policy action is necessary; or, alternatively, the pressure of unrelieved domestic demand on reduced domestic supply might stimulate inflation of the price-wage-cost structure and force policy action to restore internal equilibrium. One qualification to this picture is that, except when a credit process is beginning, there will be a flow back of interest and amortisation payments which will help to offset—perhaps completely—any new commercial credits. This assumes of course a fairly high degree of security for servicing of debts by developing countries; and this assumption has not always been entirely justified in the experience of the last twenty years.

Finally, there is the situation in which developed countries supply capital goods to developing countries as a gift or on terms which are so far from commercial arrangements that they contain a clear gift element. These arrangements withdraw supplies[2] from the donor economy without any present or future requital. They have an immediate impact on the donor economy, both

[2] This assumes that the supplies are not genuine surpluses, that is, that they are supplies for which there is a commercial market, either internally or externally.

domestically and externally, similar to the impact made by initial extensions of credit, but their impact is ultimately more severe because there is no flow-back of interest and amortisation payments; this absence of a 'revolving-fund effect' will mean that it will be harder to maintain gift or grant aid at a given level over a long period of time than it will be to maintain credits at the same level of gross outflow over the same period. Commercial credits may, of course, ultimately be no different or little different from gift or grant aid, depending on the credit-worthiness of the borrower. Some governments in the past have sought or accepted credits on a scale and for purposes which have offered little prospect that they could be repaid. Some of these debts have subsequently been written off or rescheduled.

The extent to which a developed country can extend credits or grant aid will depend on the other burdens which it carries. If it has a very small military establishment (providing therefore only minor competition with civilian demand for limited supplies), no or negligible defence establishments and defence commitments overseas, no colonies, an economy expanding in terms of employed population and productivity, a net inflow of capital and/or migrants, then it has a better chance of sustaining a considerable outflow of private capital and government loans and grants for a long period.

If a country has large defence establishments and expenditures, including large defence establishments and defence support expenditures overseas, colonial responsibilities, an economy relatively static in terms of employed population and productivity, and a high net outflow of capital and people, then it will be hard-pressed to maintain a high level of outflow of private capital and government grants and loans to developing countries for any length of time. If it attempts to do so, its own economy will suffer. The balance of payments and international reserves will deteriorate. The rate of growth of the gross national product will slow to a crawl. More and more population will be lost through migration. Capital which would otherwise have been attracted from abroad will go elsewhere. Domestic capital will lack incentive, both because of the low growth rate and because of policies of deflation which the government will feel compelled to apply in an attempt to restore equilibrium. This domestic capital will seek a happier haven elsewhere—that is, of course, if restrictions are not placed on the outflow of capital. Ultimately, some such restrictions are likely to be applied in a desperate attempt to restore equilibrium or to shore up defences against even more acute disequilibria. It is not a happy story. But it is not an unfamiliar one.

Aid and, more generally, provision of capital to developing countries is not the whole cause of the distress which some developed countries have experienced. It is only one element—one of the contributing causes of their difficulties. But this does not alter its significance. This does not change the fact that the provision of aid and capital to developing countries is, in most circumstances, an economic burden for the donor. In present circumstances, in the context of a Keynesian system, provision of aid and capital to developing countries does not offset other burdens which the donor-developed country is likely to be bearing. On the contrary, it adds to them. It may not be wholly responsible for disasters which afflict a particular developed economy. But sometimes it may be the straw which breaks the camel's back.

It is worth examining this phenomenon in a little more detail. Why can't countries which are far, far richer than they have ever been before help poor countries more than they do? Why do rich countries have so many economic difficulties? Why, in brief, are some at least of the rich countries so chronically indigent?

V
The Indigent Rich

In 1969, a respectable and conservative private research group in the United States estimated that the United States gross national product would increase from about $900 billion in 1969 to about $1500 billion in 1980, at constant prices. At about the same time, the Australian Treasurer estimated that, 'if the recent rate is maintained, our gross national product (at constant prices) would treble in twenty years'. With one important qualification about the United States, there is nothing surprising or even very newsworthy about these projections. Much the same rate of increase in gross national product is likely to be experienced by other highly developed countries. One major country—Japan —is likely, on the basis of its achievement in the last decade, to have a much higher rate of increase in her gross national product than either the United States or Australia. For all the developed countries, the norm will be a massive improvement in gross national product; only the laggards will add to their gross national product at the 2 or 3 per cent annual rate which, except for brief, boom periods was often the standard in the nineteenth and the earlier half of the twentieth century.

The increase in gross national product will be assisted, in varying degrees in the different countries, by some increase in population or, more relevantly, by some increase in the work force. But—if our projections prove to be valid—the rate of increase in the gross national product will be much higher than the rate of increase in the total population or the work force. Total population is unlikely to increase in any of the developed countries by anything like as much as 3 per cent per year and, in most of them, it is likely to be markedly less than 2 per cent. The rate of population increase in northern America between 1960 and 1969 was 1.4 per cent annually, slowing to 1.2 per cent annually in the latter part of the period from 1963 to 1969. In Western Europe, the rate of increase was 1 per cent from 1960 to 1969, slowing to 0.9 per cent from 1963 to 1969. In Japan, it was 1 per cent over the whole period, rising to 1.1 per cent from 1963 to 1969; and, in Australia and New Zealand, where the rate of increase was affected by immigration, it was 1.9 per cent annually for both the longer and the shorter period.

Given that all the developed countries are already at or near full employment, new opportunities to draw additional labour into the work force from internal sources may call for special measures. Without these special measures, the rate of increase in the work force could be the same as the rate of increase in the population, except in so far as there are changes in the age structure of the population which result in a higher or lower proportion of the total population being engaged in current production, or as new groups, such as currently unemployed women, are drawn or drawn more completely into productive employment. Generally, the prospect is that, because of higher productivity, gross national product will increase at a substantially higher rate than population or work force, so that there will be a substantial addition each year to per capita income in the developed countries.

We mentioned above that an important qualification has to be made about the prospective increase in the gross national product of the United States. This qualification relates to the sheer size of the annual accretions of United States income. In recent years —and leaving aside the induced 1970 recession—United States gross national product has been increasing at the rate of about $US50 billion annually—or about twice the gross national product of a country like Australia and considerably more than twice the gross national product of Belgium or the Netherlands. If the projections over the next ten years of additions to the United States gross national product prove to be correct, the United

States will have a gross national product in 1980 greater than that in 1970 by an amount equal to the addition of more than twenty economies the size of Australia's in 1969—or considerably more than twenty economies the size of Belgium's or the Netherlands'. Expressed in another way, the addition to gross national product in 1980 will be greater than the whole of the gross national product of all the developed market economies outside the United States in 1965 and nearly three times the combined gross national product of all the developing market economies in Asia, Africa, Latin America and Oceania in 1965. If one can imagine all these developing countries doubling their gross national product—a percentage increase just two-thirds of that forecast for Australia—in the next twenty years, their combined gross national product in 1985 will be only about two-thirds of the amount which will be *added* to the United States GNP in 1980. The prospective additions to United States production in the next ten years are, in other words, so massive that they dwarf anything which has ever been known in human experience in the past.

Potentially, existing United States national income and the accretions of the next few years provide massive resources from which to assist the developing countries. Some years ago, the United Nations accepted as a target for aid to developing countries contributions amounting to 1 per cent of the national income of the donor countries. Originally, this was conceived as 1 per cent of net national income—or was so regarded by the donor countries—and was then changed, at the Second United Nations Conference on Trade and Development in 1968, to the higher level of 1 per cent of gross national product. It will be a helpful illustration of the issues which we have in mind to apply this target to United States gross national product.

One per cent of the present (1969) United States gross national product of about $900 billion would be $9 billion. This is well above the present United States contributions to international aid, vast as those present contributions are. Perhaps we may assume for the sake of the present argument, and without probing the reasons for it, that aid contributions amounting in aggregate to $9 billion are currently beyond United States capacity. But, by 1975, United States gross national product will have increased to about $1200 billion of which 1 per cent would be $12 billion. Gross national product will have increased by about $300 billion and, out of this, the United States would be asked to set aside only $12 billion for international aid—or considerably less than that out of the additional income, because the United States is already contributing more than $US3 billion out of its present income. The upper figure of $12 billion would represent only 4 per cent of the *addition* to gross national product, 96 per cent of which would be available for additional consumption or investment within or by the United States itself. By 1980, the addition to gross national product as compared with 1969 would be $600 billion, taking gross national product to $1500 billion, of which 1 per cent would be $15 billion. Again, $15 billion would not appear to be an intolerable amount for the United States to set aside for international aid out of an addition to gross national product of $600 billion. At first glance, indeed, it would seem ungenerous, not to say unenlightened, of the United States not to rush the opportunity to make the $15 billion available.

If the opportunity were taken, it would mean that total international aid—now running at about $US13 billion from all countries (of which about half is government aid)—would rise to about $US22 billion in 1975 and $US25 billion in 1980 from the United States additions alone. Although the magnitudes would be less for other countries, the application of similar calculations to other countries would add considerable further amounts to aid, while still leaving a huge residue available for consumption and investment at home. For example, if the Australian gross national product rises from $25 billion now to, let us say, only $40 billion in 1980, then Australia would need, in the latter year, to provide $400 million if she were to meet an aid target of 1 per cent of GNP. But this would still leave more than $14½ billion out of the $15 billion added to Australia's GNP over the decade. This would surely be an aid burden almost ludicrously easy, in such affluent and dynamic circumstances, to sustain. Given the popular and political support for international aid in the donor countries, it would perhaps not be surprising if 1 per cent of GNP or even considerably more were regularly made available as international aid and if the prospect were that donors would move up to 2 per cent or 3 per cent or

4 per cent, in the next decade or so, as their affluence flowed ever more strongly.

Why don't they do it? Why do countries still not achieve their 1 per cent? Why do so many of them hedge with so many reservations any commitment to do it at any stated time in the future?

Certainly, there are good reasons and, paradoxically, they have their origins in the very Keynesian policies which have been so instrumental in creating the affluent societies of our time. In the end, the capacity of donor countries to give international aid is determined not by those countries' gross national product, but by their balance of payments and their international reserves. Let us therefore trace in more detail the path by which Keynesian policies maintain a more or less steadily increasing gross national product and per capita income and the concurrent effect of these policies on the balance of payments.

The essence of Keynesian policies is that they should achieve and maintain an equilibrium position at a level of full employment of labour and capital. If the economy shows any tendency to fall back from this equilibrium position, then an injection of spending by the government or by the banking system should be made to restore the equilibrium. If the economy overheats and the supply of money becomes so great that it outruns the capacity of the economy to produce, causing inflationary pressures, then there must—according to currently accepted theory and practice —be a reduction in government spending and/or in the amount of money made available through the banking system to restore equilibrium by bringing effective demand once again back into balance with the capacity of the economy to produce. Current theory and practice are based on the belief that this will, after some floundering perhaps, restore the optimum conditions of full employment of labour and capital, with demand and supply in harmony and the price-cost-wage situation nicely stable.

All of this is simple in theory and the capacity of governments to manoeuvre to achieve or restore balance is, again in theory, considerable. In practice, however, the first is very difficult and the second is very limited.

First of all, full employment, especially of labour, achieves a political definition, as distinct from a technical definition, over time. At the end of the Second World War, it was widely considered that a level of 4 per cent of unemployment would constitute a reasonable definition of full employment of labour. Against a background of unemployment during the thirties rising to 20 per cent and even 30 per cent and remaining, for long periods, at or above 10 per cent, it was understandable that 4 per cent should look pretty good. But, as time passed, unemployment began to settle, for long periods and in an increasing number of countries, below 4 per cent and to move towards an almost irreducible level of 1 to 2 per cent. Once people become accustomed to an unemployment level of 1 per cent, then a movement back to a rate of 2 per cent causes what is regarded as widespread distress and 3 per cent or 4 per cent comes to be regarded, in many countries, as a national disaster. While balance in the economy might seem to demand, on a technical assessment, a capacity to move unemployment over a 3 per cent range between, let us say, 1 per cent and 4 per cent, it becomes politically impossible to contemplate a range of more than 1 per cent or even, after a time, of more than ½ per cent—where a single percentage point might mean, depending on the size of the employed labour force in the particular economy, throwing out of work tens of thousands or hundreds of thousands of people.

If governments do deliberately create unemployment in an attempt to restore long-term economic stability, then they must compensate the unemployed. This applies whether governments accept that their limits of political manoeuvre extend only over a range of about ½ per cent unemployment or whether they are prepared to act more drastically. Unemployment benefits must be high and comprehensive. Those who are unfortunate enough to be 'thrown out of work' must have almost as large an income as if they had remained in employment. Especially given the narrow limits of unemployment within which, in practice, governments must operate, the reduction in consumption is consequently small and the duration of unemployment for most individuals is short. Apart from actual unemployment, there is a reduction in overtime earnings and over-award payments to labour which could—if not offset by losses of production to these factors—operate to bring the economy off the boil and the effect of this should not be neglected. But the margin for manoeuvre has nevertheless been greatly reduced, especially as consumption levels move not only within narrow but also, for the most part, within ever-narrowing limits.

Much of the above was illustrated in the message which President Nixon sent to Congress on 8 July 1969, in support of legislation for the extension of unemployment insurance. 'Unemployment insurance,' the message said, 'is an economic stabiliser. If, for example, the economy were ever to slow and unemployment were to rise, this program automatically would act to sustain personal income. This would help prevent a downturn from gathering momentum resulting from declines in purchasing power. When employment is at a high level, and great stimulation of consumer demand is unwanted, relatively little money flows into the economy from unemployment insurance. . . . '

However, if personal incomes are maintained, the withdrawal of some labour from the economy and the reduction of working hours through reduction of overtime cause lower production. Personal income is—nearly—maintained but the supply of goods to balance effective demand is at a lower level: a man gets, let us say, $30 a week for producing nothing, instead of, let us say, $60 for adding $60 or more to the gross national product. Income is down by $30 but production is down by at least $60. Multiply this by 100,000 unemployed and production will fall $156 million a year *more* than income. The net result could be both more unemployment and more inflation.

Exactly what the ultimate effect of a whole complex of movements and interactions will be is difficult to say. It will depend on the particular circumstances of each economy at the particular time. In part, it will depend on the precise measures taken by a government to damp down its own special, at least partly home-grown boom. In part, it will depend on the situation of labour at the time: the efficiency especially of marginal labour, the amount of overtime being worked, the prevalence and size of over-award payments, the relationship between employed earnings and unemployed benefits. But, whatever the exact effect of the twin movements of consumption and supply, generally it seems likely to be true that governments have gradually been moved and are still being moved to a position where, at least from the viewpoint of firm control, their options are reduced to establishing a situation somewhere between the economy being at a full-throttle boil and being at a very vigorous simmer. Even the United States—still an arch-conservative in these matters—is moving to this position, although it has not quite done so yet. Any genuine attempt to stabilise the economy *downwards* which results in more than a small percentage rise in unemployment—*highly compensated unemployment*—invites political disaster almost anywhere in the developed world outside the United States and, even in the United States, the margins have been narrowed and the 1969-70 experience will narrow them still further.

In the 1969-70 government-induced recession, the Nixon Administration went further in raising or allowing to rise the level of unemployment than would have been expected—and than might have been anticipated would have been received without outraged clamour by the community. There was disquiet and a stage was reached early in 1971 at which reflation was unavoidable; but the political impact was less than it would have been in other countries. Part of the reason for this might be the high unemployment benefits which are now available.

It was on 8 July 1969, when the unemployment rate was about 3½ per cent and before deflationary policies were implemented which pushed the rate up to about 6 per cent, that President Nixon sent to Congress the message on unemployment insurance which we quoted a short time ago. The first part of that message read:

'The Secretary of Labor is sending to the Congress today proposed legislation to extend unemployment insurance to 4,800,000 workers not now covered; to end the shortsighted restrictions that stand in the way of needed retraining efforts; and to add a federal program automatically extending the duration of benefits in periods of high unemployment. . . .'

There was nothing surprising or exceptionable in the message. It was typical of the times—and typical of the way all developed countries are now run. But, towards the end of 1969, that is, less than six months later, policies instituted by the Nixon Administration began to push unemployment up. The intention of these policies was to stop inflation by reducing demand. Demand was to be reduced by reducing personal income, which was assumed to be a function of increasing unemployment. But President Nixon had already arranged in his message to Congress that 'if unemployment were to rise', the programme of unemployment insurance 'automatically would act to sustain personal income'. He had therefore undermined in advance his capacity to attack inflation through increasing unemployment and thus reducing personal incomes. But he was more shackled in his capacity to attack inflation by these means than even this contradiction in his policies demonstrates. For his policies, if they did not reduce incomes as much as the increase in unemployment would have in an earlier period, they did reduce production. The number of unemployed shot up by more than one million in less than a year. The rate of increase in the gross national product dropped sharply. The President's Council of Economic Advisers estimated that the United States economy, in the second quarter of 1970, was operating at about 4 per cent below its potential capacity and that the real rate of growth of GNP in the third quarter was down to 1.4 per cent—or to 2.5 per cent, if the effect of the General Motors strike were excluded. Growth in the fourth quarter was probably nil. The difference between these estimates and the real rate of growth of 5 per cent or more before the advent of recessive policies was substantial; and was borne out by data showing movements in industrial production. From a peak in July 1969, the index of industrial production dropped steadily to a point 7 per cent lower in October 1970. The decline was sharper as unemployment grew (and as the General Motors strike caused further production losses). The index which stood at 173.1 in October 1969, had fallen to 166.1 in September 1970, and 162.3 in October 1970.

During the same period, retail sales continued to climb, at least in monetary terms. Sales were up from about $29.2 billion in September 1969, to $30.8 billion in September 1970, a rise of about 5 per cent. In October 1970, after allowing for the effects of the General Motors strike, they made a further small gain. Even allowing for price rises, retail sales continued in real terms at no less than the September 1969 level over the following twelve months. So that, although industrial production declined by about 7 per cent, personal incomes, sustained, *inter alia*, by higher social-security payments and higher wages, remained sufficiently strong to push up retail sales in monetary terms and at least to prevent any decline in real terms.

PERSONAL INCOME

Source: *The Wall Street Journal,* 4 December 1970

The two accompanying charts showing the simultaneous upward movement in retail sales and downward movement in
industrial production illustrate vividly the increasing inflationary
strains to which the economy had been exposed. The net effect
of the Nixon Administration's policies of increasing unemployment and thus reducing production, while at the same time
maintaining personal incomes through social-security payments,
was not to curb inflation but to accentuate it. The trade unions,
in their turn, made more militant by the deteriorating labour
market and seeking 'compensation' by wage rises and other
improved conditions, made a further contribution to inflation,
both through newly negotiated industrial agreements and through
the strikes which they sometimes used to achieve them. This
1970 United States experience suggests that, at best, governments
of advanced economies applying fairly advanced Keynesian
policies, have very limited room to manoeuvre in restoring

stability at the upper level of employment of the economy, if they use the traditional means of damping down demand and creating unemployment. At anything less than the best, governments by acting in this way might only intensify the very evils they are trying to eradicate.

But even if the limited room to manoeuvre is enough, government action must also be timely; indeed, it must be timely with a precision quite unprecedented. If the boil of the economy becomes too great, then it will be extremely difficult, if not impossible, to take action which will satisfactorily bring it back to a very vigorous simmer, without grossly violating some of the attitudes to acceptable rates of unemployment, slow and negative growth rates, and all the rest which now have become part of the conventional pattern of politico-economic thinking in developed countries. The result will be that the boil will continue with results which will be—and here we come to the crux of the matter with which this argumentation was initially directed to deal—with results which will be disastrous for the balance of payments.

A full-employment, high-growth equilibrium has to be one which is in balance both domestically and externally. Domestically, it must avoid inflation on the one hand, and unacceptable levels of unemployment and other unused economic resources on the other. Externally, it must avoid either a chronic surplus or a chronic deficit in the balance of payments; especially the latter, because recent experience has shown that some countries can live most comfortably with a chronic surplus, which, indeed, yields advantages of external strength, prestige and manoeuvrability in terms both of external and domestic politico-economic policies. A chronic deficit, on the other hand, compels a change or modification of domestic and/or external policies since erosion of international reserves cannot be allowed to persist indefinitely.

Equilibrium in the domestic position is, as this implies, not separate from and independent of equilibrium in the external position. A real and satisfactory equilibrium means equilibrium in both. A disturbance in the equilibrium of one will, sooner or later, lead to disequilibrium in the other. How does this come about?

The essence of the optimum equilibrium under a Keynesian

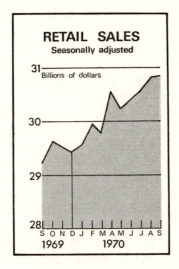

Source: The New York Times, 10 November 1970

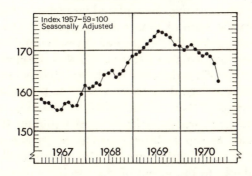

Source: The Wall Street Journal, 18 November 1970

system is that aggregate expenditure on consumption and investment should equal aggregate output of capital and consumer goods of the economy under conditions of full employment. If expenditure is maintained but production falls—because of droughts or other national disasters, a fall in employment, etc. —the resulting excess of expenditure will cause a rise in imports. If expenditure is reduced while production is maintained, the excess production will, where practicable, tend to find its way into external markets.

There are other possible variations. If aid is given to developing countries and part of this aid is made available as free exchange, then the giving of aid will, to the extent that it is spent abroad, have a deflationary effect on the donor economy: purchasing power will be skimmed off the donor economy and applied to increasing expenditure in some external market or markets. So long as United States aid programmes provided for substantial off-shore purchases, the United States economy was affected in this way. While external economic and technical aid was running at, say, $4 billion a year and only 75 per cent was spent on United States goods and services, then $1 billion a year was withdrawn from the United States economy. The budget would need, in these circumstances, to show a deficit of $1 billion if the joint effect of aid and taxation were not to have any deflationary effect on the economy.

There are other effects. If aid is given in conditions of Keynesian equilibrium, resources are withdrawn from the domestic economy which must then be replaced by imports. Aid—whether it is given in the form of grants or repayable credits—then becomes a debit against the balance of payments and, in isolation, goes to reduce international reserves. Whether the donor economy can sustain this effect depends on the particular circumstances of the economy. If the donor economy is itself a substantial net importer of capital, then the aid which it gives may not, in the short term at least, endanger its external liquidity. If the donor economy tends to run a chronic surplus on its balance of payments, then it can sustain external aid—plus other unrequited external outlays—to the extent of the surplus.

A country is likely to be a chronic creditor only in special circumstances and the term 'chronic' will therefore cover only the period during which these special circumstances persist. Chronic creditors are, in this sense, as much children of their time as chronic debtors. A country might be a chronic creditor because its currency is undervalued; because its external payments position has been strengthened by, for example, large discoveries of oil or minerals; because it has suddenly given up large external commitments (for example, as a result of decolonisation) and the economy adjusts only slowly to the luxury of this new freedom from unrequited burdens; or because other countries have put themselves or allow themselves to remain in the position of chronic debtors, a corollary of which is that there will be somewhere or other equivalent chronic creditors. These causes are not exhaustive; rather are they illustrative.

The important point that we want to make here is that a country's status as a chronic creditor or a chronic debtor is not a God-given blessing or a divinely-bestowed cross, but an outcome of special circumstances which can be identified and which are often—indeed, usually—the outcome of political, social or economic policies which have been deliberately embarked upon or which have been inherited from the past. Within this general framework, it can be said that the capacity of a developed economy to sustain what might be termed a world role—no matter how rich, how high its per capita income, or how rapid its rate of economic growth—is very limited. The sort of world role which might be envisaged for a major power would entail the following outlays:

1 A substantial net outflow of private and government capital;
2 Substantial contributions of economic and technical aid, both bilaterally and multilaterally;
3 Provision of defence aid and almost certainly the stationing of substantial armed forces in allied countries;
4 Loss of population through stationing of armed forces as under 3, through provision of personnel in association with direct capital investment and economic and—especially—technical aid.

The relationship between the balance of current account trade (including services) and the size of international reserves will determine how large these outlays may be and for how long they may be allowed to persist. This is the relationship which is important, and *not* the relationship between the outlays listed above and a country's gross national product or the annual addition to that gross national product.

This may be translated into concrete terms. At present, United States foreign reserves are of the order of $US13 billion. For many years—about a decade, although the extent of the movement has been irregular—these reserves have been declining. At the start of the sixties, they were of the order of $US20 billion. In the intervening years, although gross national product and per capita income in the United States have increased massively—in fact, to a quite unprecedented extent in absolute terms—foreign reserves have been drastically reduced and at the end of the sixties are less than three-quarters of their level at the beginning of the decade. We have said that this has happened although gross national product and per capita income have increased massively; in fact, the decline in reserves has been, in a sense, a reflex of this massive increase in GNP and per capita income.

We must also bear in mind that United States reserves have continued to decline despite two special countervailing factors. The first is that reserves have been held at a level higher than would otherwise have been the case because of the status of the United States dollar as a reserve currency. Many countries have been prepared to hold a large part of their foreign reserves and accretions to those reserves not in the form of gold but in the form of United States dollars. This practice has persisted, although the degree of other countries' willingness to hold their reserves in the form of dollars has declined as the dollar has weakened. France, for political as well as—or despite—economic reasons, was the leader or, at least, the most public and dramatic opponent of the practice of holding foreign reserves in the form of dollars or other reserve currencies; but other countries have also tended to be less enthusiastic than before about holding their reserves in dollars. This, plus the weakening of the dollar from more concrete causes, has caused a quickening erosion of United States reserves.

The other special factor is that, as the level of United States reserves has fallen, the United States Government has taken action to improve its balance-of-payments position and thus to slow down or reverse erosion of its reserves. It has made strenuous efforts to expand its exports and to reduce American tourist expenditures and, for example, expenditure on diplomatic representation abroad. It has placed restraints on the outflow of private capital. The level of economic and technical aid, although it has remained high, has tended to level out in monetary terms and, in real terms, has already fallen from its high point earlier in the sixties. The United States Government has also tried to reduce its defence outlays overseas and its defence aid, although any success which has attended these efforts has been more than offset by the huge increase in overseas defence expenditures attendant upon the war in Viet-Nam. The reduction of forces in Viet-Nam since 1969 is in harmony with economic as with political imperatives. President Nixon's 'real problem', said one commentator in 1969, 'is the gap that has opened up between the fact that the Americans now take a greater interest in the outside world than they have ever done—like every country with television plus a free press—and the fact that they seem to be less willing than at any time since 1941 to back up this interest with the conventional tools for influencing events: that is, with money and soldiers. It is not just that so many of them dislike the Viet-Nam war. The problem is that the Viet-Nam experience has made a substantial number of Americans turn their backs on the ideas that have shaped the past twenty years of American foreign policy.'[1] The Viet-Nam war did not, by itself, cause a revision of American attitudes, but it crystallised attitudes which had been forming and would have formed anyway; and it made clearer and more convincing and more immediate the imperatives of United States withdrawal from, or reduction of, many of its political, strategic and economic involvements overseas.

Despite all these efforts, deficits in the United States balance of payments persist and so does the trend towards a further reduction of the foreign reserves. If the war in Viet-Nam were to end—and especially if the American forces were quickly re-absorbed into non-defence production at home—this would provide major relief to the balance of payments. Just how much is difficult to say. It could mean the conversion of the payments

[1] *The Economist*, London, 2 August 1969, p. 11

deficit into a surplus. However, this would assume that there were no new external outlays to replace the savings from the ending of the war. It could too mean an end to domestic inflation; but this would depend on whether the men and other economic resources released from the war were used to increase civilian production and bring civilian production into harmony with civilian demand.

During the course of the war, many references have been made to the United States Government's intention to apply the resources now used to wage war in Viet-Nam to economic aid for developing countries, especially in South-east Asia. This just can't be done. Or it can't be done unless there is a fundamental change in the United States and the world international payments situation; or unless the United States achieves a rearrangement of its overseas outlays which permits increased aid to these countries.

This is so because the expenditures and use of men in Viet-Nam are a major element, not of equilibrium, but of disequilibrium in the United States economy. If the present level of aggregate United States outlays were allowed to persist, United States foreign reserves would disappear entirely. The further expansion of gross national product, the accumulation of domestic wealth and the increase in per capita income will not prevent the reserves from draining away. If anything, the persistence of this domestic dynamism—if it is used and abused as it is now—will only accelerate the drain in foreign reserves.

As we discussed before, it is politically impracticable to reduce, except within narrowing limits, employment, consumption, the accumulation of wealth and the increase in per capita income. Inbuilt mechanisms will maintain the level of consumption and no government, whatever its complexion, will find it politically practicable—even in the United States—to reduce too far levels of employment of labour and other economic factors of production; by the time of the elections in November 1970, United States unemployment had already been increased by deliberate deflationary policy as far as the community was prepared to tolerate. Implicitly or explicitly politicians and others were saying: 'Any level of unemployment is too high. Every American is entitled to a job.' In any event, the maintenance of consumption by inbuilt mechanisms would make reduction of employment very nearly futile or worse. Production would be reduced by so much more than consumption that the enemy of inflation which government policies were aimed to reduce would only be intensified by further increases in unemployment. Already by the elections of November 1970, it was obvious that growing unemployment was accompanied by growing inflation in the United States.

Given this, the only theoretical variables which, in practice, can be varied by government action are, first, aggregate production and, second, overseas expenditure. For the moment, we will leave aside the possibility of government action to increase aggregate production. In the end, this might be the most important element in the solution to Keynesian disequilibrium of the kind which the United States—and some other developed countries, including Britain—are experiencing at the present time. But, first, let us look at the prospects for rectifying the disequilibrium by reducing overseas expenditure.

The greatest single overseas expenditure is on commodity imports. Can these be reduced? In theory, they can and they can be in practice to some extent too. But expenditure on imports cannot be reduced to any significant degree because their reduction would lower the level of supply in relation to purchasing power and so intensify domestic inflation—the other trap besides balance-of-payments deficit into which the economy in this situation stands in constant danger of falling. Between the scylla of external deficits and the charybdis of domestic inflation the only course open to the United States Government acting by itself is to reduce external outlays under such major headings as overseas capital movements, economic and technical aid and external defence expenditure and support.

The United States is not uniquely confronted with this dilemma. Other countries—at some time or other, all those countries applying mature Keynesian policies—might experience it too or might have already done so. In particular, Britain has gone through the same experience; the differences are only of details, of timing and of degree. Britain's experience came earlier, has lasted longer and has been more acute. Immediately after the Second World War, Britain was one of the first countries to apply Keynesian policies. She has maintained a high level of employment and economic activity ever since. The periods of deflation, imposed by successive governments principally to meet successive payments crises within an almost constantly difficult external situation, have been mild compared with the inter-war period and mild compared even with the United States especially before the effective advent of Keynesian policies there from 1961 onwards. However, Britain's world role, though constantly shrinking, has had to be maintained to some extent throughout the period since 1945. Colonial responsibilities, including the heavy expenditures and diversion largely of skilled personnel which go with them, have been shed only slowly and some of them still persist. Some responsibilities have carried over into the post-colonial phase of many former British colonies; these have related especially to economic and technical aid and, in some cases, have involved even a continuation of external defence expenditures. There is nothing very unusual in this. It is difficult to chop off colonial commitments—the rather sad and discouraging exception was former French Guinea—precisely at the date of political independence.

Quite apart from continuing colonial and post-colonial responsibilities, Britain had formed some habits before the Keynesian era which she has found it extremely difficult to break. For example, Britain had been one of the world's major exporters of capital ever since the Industrial Revolution and, despite all the payments vicissitudes of the last generation, this export of capital has continued. British investment overseas, much of which had had to be repatriated during the Second World War, has been built up again since and is now higher than it has ever been. Again, British emigration—a centuries-old habit—has persisted since the Second World War. These emigrants have not only represented a loss of British investment, for example, in education and welfare, but have also taken personal and sometimes other capital with them to the countries of emigration; they have included a high proportion of people in the most productive age-groups and a high proportion of professional and other skilled personnel; and they have reduced both supply and demand—but, for reasons already given, they have probably reduced supply more than demand—in the British economy. For Britain, with her shrinking but continuing world role, the effect of emigration has been intensified by the withdrawal from the economy (in a way which amounts to *de facto* emigration), of large numbers of colonial administrators and other personnel, defence personnel in the remaining colonies and in ex-colonial countries under continuing defence arrangements as well as, for example, in Western Europe under NATO. In addition, unrequited expenditures in the colonies or under post-colonial arrangements have placed a burden on the balance of payments and on international reserves similar in the short-term—that is, before interest and amortisation payments can effect a distinction—to the outflow of private capital.

Britain's postwar economic problems have not fundamentally been soluble by deflation or devaluation but—leaving aside for the moment possible increases in production—by an end to colonial and post-colonial responsibilities and a drastic reduction of, or an end to, emigration and defence outlays and the outflow of capital. Realisation of the first would have greatly assisted in the realisation of the other three, and would have tended to establish a situation in which net immigration would replace net emigration, and a net inflow of capital would replace the present net outflow.

But the essential point to be made here is not how to solve Britain's economic problems, but rather that even the richest and strongest economies—and by most standards, Britain as well as the United States comes into that category—have only limited resources which, under modern economic policies, they can devote to a world role. In this sense, the rich and the very rich become surprisingly poor. And the more quickly they become richer, the poorer they sometimes seem to become in terms of their capacity to sustain a world role. The United States was much better able to sustain a world role during the fifties than during the sixties, even though its national income and its annual rate of growth were much smaller in the earlier period. Now that it is fantastically rich in terms of gross national product and (even in poor growth years) annual additions to gross national product, it is forced to husband its external resources and to curb its external expenditures as though it had suddenly become poor and shabby and down at heel. Senator Fulbright, a distinguished politician of this country with the highest per capita income in human history, speaking in 1970 at a time when that per capita income was at a record level and still rising, when aggregate national income was at a record level and still rising, when the United States economy was, as we have seen, adding two Australian economies to itself every year, could say publicly that the Australian economy was financially in better shape than the United States; and he could be believed. The rich have become the indigent. To become rich—in a way that will most benefit those who need their support—they seem to need to become poorer or at least to slow down their rush to greater and greater riches. This is a paradox which neither those foreigners who need to be sustained nor those citizens who feel that economic power should be more capable of exercising itself or being exercised, always see with the clarity which would seem to be desirable.

There is perhaps a way around the paradox and this we shall discuss elsewhere. But, for the moment, one point already made must be re-emphasised. That is, that it is not only just some developed countries which, though rich, get into an economic morass. The indigence of the rich is a disease which all the rich are in danger of sharing—not all of them simultaneously, but each of them at one time or another. Britain and the United States have not been guilty of any special incompetence, nor are they paying a penalty for any special viciousness in their economic policy. On the contrary, if we are to judge them in moral terms, we must acknowledge the unprecedented generosity, especially of the United States, in helping their economically weaker brothers throughout the world. Sometimes this generosity has been obviously tied to political benefits which the United States had hoped to gain. But often the political or economic benefits have been negligible and sometimes negative.

Britain and the United States are, therefore, not particularly incompetent or vicious. What has happened to them could happen to other developed countries, including, for example, Australia. Indeed, Australia's future situation might come to approximate, in quite startling measure, to that of the United States and to that which, in lesser and declining degree, still confronts Britain today. Especially as the United States limits its world role and reduces its unrequited external outlays, Australia will almost certainly be called upon to make increasing and politically unavoidable outlays of external economic and technical aid. But, even more than that—unless the concept of 'Fortress Australia' proves to be both feasible and politically acceptable, and even, to some extent, if it does—Australia is likely to have to bear heavy strategic expenditures, whether for her own forces or for those of her allies. The burdens of those countries like the United States and Britain, which will have withdrawn to prosper more fully, might have to be borne by those countries like Australia which cannot withdraw. Bearing in mind the economic experience of Britain and the United States, Australia will have to enjoy some special advantages if she is both to bear these burdens and to maintain the sort of high employment Keynesian policies—with deflationary policies when the boom gets out of hand—which she has applied in the past. She will need to maintain or improve on the present high rate of capital inflow; she will need to maintain or improve her present export/import performance; and in particular, she will need to maintain the phenomenal advantage in her balance of payments of which the minerals boom during the sixties has brought such great promise. If one or all of these were to fail, Australia might find that unrequited outlays on aid and defence were at such a level that they were inconsistent either with the maintenance of a high level of economic activity and consequently high growth rates within Australia, or with the maintenance of equilibrium in the balance of payments under relatively free market conditions. In those circumstances, only a fundamentally new approach, which will be suggested later, could restore consistency and equilibrium.

But, while the difficulties of Britain and the United States could become the difficulties of Australia and other developed countries, it does not have to happen that way. If certain policies are modified in certain ways, some difficulties will be avoided. Some of those countries which, in recent years, have not shared the difficulties of Britain and the United States have pursued policies very different from these two countries. They have done so not entirely because of any special vision or genius but partly at least because their historical background was different. They had, in a sense, fewer options, but the options they did have were better suited to the economic context of the time than the options which were denied them. One of these countries

—the outstanding example among those which have avoided the economic tribulations of Britain and the United States—is Japan.

In a recent review of *The Japanese Challenge* by Robert Guillain, Takashi Oka[1] likened Japan to 'a Frankenstein who has learned the techniques of the West without really imbibing its spirit. This Frankenstein undersells German cameras in Germany, Swiss watches in Switzerland and American cars in America, while keeping foreign merchandise from flooding his own domestic markets through a cunning combination of laws and shadowy "administrative guidance". Meanwhile, he sucks dry developed and less developed nations alike of their iron and copper, their oil and their bauxite, in a relentless world-wide search for raw materials to feed the insatiable maws of his constantly expanding furnaces and factories.'

Perhaps—leaving aside a few extravagant and occasionally emotive and pejorative adjectives—this is a fair description of the Japanese economy in the late 1960's and the beginning of the 1970's. At least it gives a valid impression of its dynamism. But elsewhere Mr Ota describes some other features and characteristics of the Japanese economy without realising or explicitly proclaiming their causal connection with the terrifying dynamism which he has adumbrated so vividly. He says that *The Japanese Challenge* is a 'warm, provocative, basically optimistic analysis of a restlessly energetic yet inward-looking people, over 100-million strong, cooped up on four narrow islands that history and defeat in World War II left them as their only patrimony. . . .' The author's major thesis is persuasive: that the Japanese have reached their present position by their own hard work and by a kind of consensus that, as he phrases it, they should seek "greatness without the bomb". Unlike France under President de Gaulle, Mr Guillain implies, Japan has chosen economic strength while relying on the United States and the Soviet Union to provide the balance of terror upon which rests the fragile stability of the world, leaving the Japanese (and any other like-minded country) to pursue economic greatness without the clanking burden of a heavy military establishment.' There is a great deal in this description which explains the Japanese success story.

Japan, like Germany, often seems to have a special mystique

1 *The New York Times Book Review*, 25 October 1970

—in her case, perhaps a sort of oriental magic—for success with a modern economy. She hasn't. All that has happened is that history and circumstances have combined to give Japan all those attitudes and conditions which a country needs for economic success at the present time. Those attitudes and conditions are:

1 Acceptance of material goals, as well as the value of capital, education, research and hard work;
2 Freedom (not by their own choice but by military defeat) from any colonial burdens and responsibilities;
3 Freedom (originally not by their own choice, although they have come so far to accept the ideal as their own) from military ambitions and from the burdens, distortions and disequilibria which result from heavy defence responsibilities;
4 An intense, introspective interest in their own domestic economic development;
5 Overseas investment limited as far as possible to facilitating the provision of raw materials for the Japanese economy or otherwise directly benefiting the Japanese economy (for example, investment in Australian iron and coal mines to supply Japanese industry);
6 A refusal to be drawn any more than is unavoidable into unrequited external outlays on economic and technical aid for developing countries;
7 The provision of constant stimuli to domestic *production*, so that monetary and demand expansion can be met—and the effort is made, by restriction of imports, to have it met—without intolerable disequilibria, either in the domestic cost, price and wage structure or in the external balance;
8 Finally, a large population highly concentrated in a small area, thus presenting ready-made the sort of socio-economic arrangement suited to development of concentrated secondary and, even more importantly, of tertiary industry towards which other economies, more diffuse and scattered, are still striving to move.

Perhaps there is embedded in the Japanese success story the secrets of economic success for other developed countries. This success has come about, as we have already suggested, not because they have had any special mystique or magic or even any genius of perception not shared by others. Some of the elements in their success they would not have chosen themselves. Nor would other countries. The crushing defeat of 1945 and the horrors of Hiroshima were the penalty of miscalculation. But, in retrospect, the miscalculation of 1941 may have been one of the most profitable miscalculations in history. Nothing can ever erase the horrors of Hiroshima but, in so far as the experience of nuclear bombing, in the context of total and humiliating defeat, turned the Japanese personality away from war and empire, it provided one of the most important elements in Japan's spectacular rise to economic greatness in the last quarter-century. There are other elements too in the Japanese success story which deserve identification and analysis because of their relevance to other developed economies.

But we shall defer that until a little later. At the moment, we want to go on to consider the promptings to anti-colonialism and then to describe how the economic policies of the developed countries since 1945—policies which have themselves been a vital element in ending colonialism—have gradually and fairly rapidly resulted in a division of the world economy into two groups of countries with largely opposing interests.

VI
The Promptings to Anti-colonialism

Colonialism was the creation of the economic interest of its time. So was its ending. Not entirely of course. No story of a major movement is ever as simple as that. And even if it were, it would quickly become surrounded by myths to obscure and perhaps to overwhelm its substance.

These myths, once created, acquire a life of their own. They become not merely a mist obscuring the real truth but a political, social and economic reality with a driving force of its own. Do the myths ever operate in opposition to the reality? Probably not, if a comprehensive view is taken of a phase or movement in human history. Probably the thrust of the myths coincides with what is reality for the dominant and most progressive human communities at the time they are created. But they will not necessarily coincide—or coincide to the same degree—for all communities at the same time. Some European countries became addicted to colonialism early; some felt the urge much later; and some never really experienced it at all. The same variety of response has characterised the movement to end colonialism. Some were eager to get out early; some fought against it but at length capitulated; and some have still not abandoned colonialism nor their belief in their real national interest in it.

We don't need to be Marxists or Imperialists to concede that colonialism brought the colonial powers some advantages. These were not of the same kind or magnitude for all colonies or for all colonial powers. But, as a generality, colonies provided useful markets, useful supply sources, outlets for investment and labour, and management opportunities for nationals of the colonial powers. In certain situations—especially when production tended to outrun demand and during cyclical depressions—the existence of these colonies could be, or were thought to be, of considerable importance.

In certain other situations, their importance was less; and there must have been some colonies which were always an economic liability to the colonial power, although they may have brought some benefits to individual nationals, and some satisfaction to national ambition. Especially to the extent that the more obvious, imperialist forms of exploitation disappeared and trade and investment opportunities ceased to depend on nationality, the economic liabilities of a colonial system became more and more apparent. Pressures to dismantle the colonial system—pressures which began to operate from about the end of the First World War—probably came first from political, social, and humanitarian motives and did not initially have, or seem to have, their origin in economic change. These non-economic motives were probably always dominant for those with an awareness of their positive promptings to action.[1] In so far as pressure groups existed to exert influence in favour of colonial policy, these groups consisted of individuals and companies deriving benefit from certain territories and therefore anxious to protect their interests; they could do this most effectively and with maximum assurance by maintaining the colonial power's sovereignty. The cost—the liabilities of colonialism—were of a national kind and here other elements —including national prestige—entered to weaken pressure for decolonisation. At least until very recently, for example, in Britain in dealing with residue territories, economic interests seem never to have been used positively to advocate dismantling the colonial system. But, as economic interest in the colonies declined, the way was made clearer for political, social and humanitarian pressures for decolonisation to achieve their purpose.

[1] British Ministers and officials dismantling or trying to dismantle the last of the British colonial system are much more conscious of economic factors (even economic imperatives) than were their counterparts at the time of, let us say, the granting of independence to India more than twenty years ago.

However, if no national economic liabilities had been incurred under colonialism, and especially if, on the contrary, the colonial powers had derived vital economic advantage, both national and sectional, from their possession of colonies, they would have held much more tenaciously to their colonies than they did. Some colonies did indeed achieve their independence through force of arms and some colonial powers gave up their sovereignty only because, through temporary or continuing weakness, they were no longer able to exert it. But, in the perspective of history, the surprising thing may be, not that the colonial system persisted so long, but that the colonial powers gave up their territories so quickly and so readily in the two decades after the end of the Second World War. Where a colonial power, such as Portugal, has been determined, it is surprising how long it has been able to hold on to its colonial possessions and how ineffective international pressures of various kinds have been. It may also be significant that Portugal, the colonial power which has held most tenaciously to its colonial possessions, is a European power which has participated least in the great economic advances which have moved most of the countries bordering the North Atlantic. In other words, the motives and the self-interest which caused other colonial powers to decolonise or at least to relax their resistance to decolonisation, have not yet begun to operate in Portugal because its economy still belongs, in effect, to an earlier period of European history—a period whose economic promptings to colonialism carried European sovereignty to almost every tiny corner of the world.

Certainly the loss of colonies has caused the colonial powers remarkably little distress. Indeed, the evidence is that, on the contrary, countries which have lost their colonies have subsequently enjoyed conditions of quite unusual dynamism and economic growth. The major colonial powers in 1945 were Britain, France, the Netherlands and Belgium.

Britain began[2] its process of decolonisation shortly after the Second World War in 1945. For a quarter of a century the process has been going on. More than a score of countries have

---

[2] This leaves aside the process by which Britain gave independence to colonies *of its own people*—Canada, Australia, South Africa, New Zealand —before the Second World War.

been granted their independence. Only a few minor colonial territories now remain under the British flag. But, even so, the process, after a quarter of a century, is still not quite complete. Britain remains—unwillingly—a colonial power.

It was also in 1945 that Britain adopted Keynesian policies of economic stability. Full employment was an accepted goal of government policy from the end of the Second World War. The various British political parties have expressed their support for full employment with differing degrees of emphasis and differing motivations; but all governments of whatever complexion have accepted full employment and have applied the fiscal and monetary measures necessary to sustain it.

Britain has thus constantly and intensively applied the Keynesian policies of the new era while still carrying—though in declining degree—the burdens of the older, pre-Keynesian, colonialist era. The contradictions inherent in this situation are a measure of vicissitudes through which Britain has passed in the last generation. True, the people of Britain—not just some of them but virtually all of them—have been vastly better off since 1945 than they were in the 1930's or any earlier period. But the economy has been in almost constant disequilibrium, especially in its balance of payments and has been almost constantly seeking and trying out expedients of economic policy to correct a situation which needs more fundamental measures.

Colonies have not been the sole cause of Britain's troubles. Modern economies are more complex than that; and so are the national histories with which most countries are, depending on the circumstances, blessed or shackled. Britain has a long tradition of overseas migration and investment, both of which are of doubtful value to her in the Keynesian stage of her development. And she has continued to be shackled with the heritage of her former status as the world's greatest power. Especially in the years immediately after the Second World War, this was a heritage which she found it difficult to give up. And the Conservative Party—or some of it—shared this reluctance even into the 1970's and until the reality, which sprang from the responsibilities of government, finally compelled it to surrender. Even then, while it surrendered the substance, it clung nostalgically to the shadow of Britain's heritage as a country with a world role and world responsibilities. Unfortunately a world role is expensive both in terms of maintenance of a defence establishment at home and in terms of the stationing of defence forces and giving defence support overseas. In a low-consumption, low-employment economy, these defence burdens can—paradoxically —be sustained. In the high-consumption, high-employment economy of the Keynesian era, they introduce disequilibria of internal inflation and external payments which ultimately compel some fundamental adjustments. That is what the debate in Britain in the late 1960's and early 1970's on, for example, the East of Suez policy, was all about.

The pressures of Keynesian policies have compelled not merely an acceptance but increasingly an enthusiasm for decolonisation and for abandonment of a world role by Britain. Some attitudes remain. The attachment to overseas investment was maintained by the Wilson Labour Government throughout its term of office from 1964 until 1970 and British overseas investment increased during that period.[3] It increased while the economic growth rate at home remained one of the lowest among the developed countries, while deflationary policies forced down employment and production, and while such desperate expedients as an 'incomes policy' proved their uselessness. Restrictions on capital flows were imposed and intensified from time to time, but the rate of flow remained high, and the level of British overseas investment at the end of the period was quite astronomical in the light of the payments tribulations Britain had been through.

But at least any lingering affection for colonialism is dead. Britain has been freed of most of her colonies and she is determind to free herself of what is left as soon as she can. When the process is completed, she will then have cleared away at least some of the pre-Keynesian debris which has caused such strains in implementing Keynesian policies.

The experience of the other colonial powers has been, fundamentally, the same as Britain's, although it has been less complex. Britain was the largest colonial power; she was, during the nineteenth century and much of the twentieth, the world's greatest power, with the heaviest, most responsible and most expensive

[3] Private British overseas investment seems to have amounted to £stg.2871 million in the six years from 1964 to 1969 inclusive.

world political and defence role; and she was, for nearly two hundred years, one of the world's greatest overseas investors. France, the Netherlands and Belgium shared some of Britain's characteristics as a world power, but none of them had those characteristics in anything like a comparable degree.

France, which came closest to Britain as a world power, shared most of her economic troubles until 1958. Its colonial empire was less extensive but her colonial wars, especially in Indo-China and Algeria, were much more debilitating. On the other hand, the French Government applied Keynesian policies rather later and with less intensity than did Britain. However, France in the period 1945 to 1958 was in essentially the same position as Britain, with a serious contradiction between her continuing colonial burdens and her new Keynesian policies of stability and growth.

More than any other country, France's decolonisation can be attached to a single date. In 1958, France granted independence to most of her colonies and ended the disastrous conflict in Algeria. Almost overnight, a tremendous burden was lifted from the French economy. French soldiers—not all of them, but most of them—returned home. French burdens for colonial adminis- tration and development were reduced. They were not eliminated overnight and some of the most obvious colonial assistance, such as direct budget support for some small African countries, con- tinued into and, in declining degree, throughout the 1960's. In one or two cases, French 'intervention forces' remained to sustain a shaky government in power against actual or potential rebel forces.

But, by and large, a great burden was lifted from the French economy in 1958. Suddenly, she was rich and stable. Everything which had seemed impossible for decades suddenly seemed dead easy. Britain, which had, for decades, seemed a classic of stability and good government by the standards of the French, suddenly seemed like a stumbling incompetent unable to achieve that economic growth and payments surplus which the French could now manage with the greatest of ease.

But the French did not learn their lesson. Perhaps they were human enough to think that their good fortune was a belated but natural reward for French genius. Perhaps they thought that de Gaulle was responsible for it all; certainly, in part, he was,

anyway. Or perhaps some thought that the sudden good fortune
was partly due to something which was only partly French. That
was the Common Market.

But, if they knew what had brought about their sudden good
fortune, they did little to preserve it. De Gaulle promptly set out
to make France a great power and to give it, potentially, something of a world role again. He engaged in heavy defence spending; he gave France a nuclear bomb; and he spent money on
aircraft and rocketry intended to enhance the national image.
Though France had given independence to her African colonies,
she continued to maintain a close interest in them. Aid programmes were maintained and were used, *inter alia*, to support
a French administrative and policy apparatus within some of the
post-colonial arrangements. Government grants and loans and
private investment were used to maintain French influence in the
former colonies; and their markets were, by various devices, safe-
guarded for the French exporter. Some of the shaky African
governments had understandings with or direct armed support
from de Gaulle to keep them in power. French troops intervened
in Gabon in 1964 and French troops were kept in Chad throughout the 1960's and fought against the rebel tribesmen in the north
of this large and mainly desert republic. France still kept some
of her colonial possessions, mainly in the Pacific, including New
Caledonia and Tahiti.

As a result of these policies, France provided a greater proportion of her gross national income for aid to developing
countries than any other donor country during the period right
through from 1958 to 1970. She provided a much higher proportion than the declining percentage of Britain and the United
States. Those countries which were so loud in their clamour for
more and more aid for developing countries—such as the Scan-
dinavian countries and the Netherlands—were miserly in the
percentage of their respective GNP's which they devoted to
foreign aid compared with France.

But France paid the penalty. For a decade, the going was great.
From 1958 to 1968, almost all the indicators were good and the
gradual erosion of the benefits of 1958 by policies which went
against the lessons of 1958 passed by unnoticed. Then, in 1968,
French greatness collapsed with a suddenness which matched

its creation a decade earlier. French genius suddenly looked like French ineptitude. And a new French Government set about searching for a new formula for success.

Colonialism was not the sole cause of France's economic difficulties before 1958. Nor was its substantial abandonment in 1958 solely responsible for the great improvements in economic growth and stability afterwards. But the evidence is that colonialism or its substantial abandonment was an important element in both these situations; and the evidence is that France will continue to have economic difficulties until she makes her abandonment of colonialism and neo-colonialism more complete.

The Belgians and the Dutch are no cleverer or more virtuous or more businesslike than the British or the French. They have had, historically, no national genius which the British and the French have lacked. The Dutch are rather more like the British than the French; half of the Belgians are like the Dutch and the British and the other half are like the French. But it is all pretty much of a muchness. Therefore, it could be instructive to have a look at the experience of the Dutch and the Belgians and to try to assess the reasons which, at the moment at least, make the Netherlands and Belgium strong, stable economies while France and Britain appear unstable and enfeebled.

Neither Holland nor Belgium has any world role. Neither has any substantial colonies any longer. Holland lost her empire in the East Indies in the later 1940's; and Belgium precipitately gave independence to the Congo in 1960. Holland still has a few West Indian islands included in the Netherlands Realm; but they are so small that they have no political or military or economic significance in a national sense. The Netherlands' and Belgium's only defence commitments are for their own defence and as members of NATO; they have shown a hearty reluctance to extend these defence commitments even, for example, under the disturbing impact of the Russian invasion of Czechoslovakia in 1968. Both the Netherlands and Belgium have been loud in their support of economic and technical aid to developing countries; but their performance, expressed as a percentage of their gross national product, has so far been poor compared with some other developed countries, such as France and Australia, and falls far short of the 1 per cent of gross national product which has now been widely accepted as a quantitative target for aid by the developed countries.

The loss of colonies hasn't hurt them. When the Netherlands lost what is now Indonesia in 1947-48, she was still in the throes of post-war reconstruction. So were most of the other countries of Europe. The beneficial impact of the loss of Indonesia was therefore obscured. We can only speculate how much more difficult this reconstruction would have been for the Netherlands and how difficult growth and stability would still be for them if Indonesia had not won its independence twenty years ago. Even West Irian, surrendered with such reluctance, would have been a burden for the Netherlands if she still had a responsibility for its development. As it is, she has not. Perhaps it is too easy to slip into the fallacy of *post hoc ergo propter hoc*. But at least the facts are clear. The Netherlands has lost her colonies, has no world role and has a relatively small defence burden. She gives aid, but not too much. She invests overseas but as much or more is invested in the Netherlands by foreigners. And the result? She is rich and strong and happy; in almost every respect, she has never had it so good.

So it has been with Belgium. Until 1960, when she surrendered the Congo, Belgium had been the sick man of Europe. She was late in applying Keynesian policies. She was therefore able to hold on to the Congo and she thought she *needed* to hold on to the Congo. She was still, in some measure, living in the pre-Keynesian, colonial era.

Then things changed. By 1960, most Western European countries had gone Keynesian and even the United States was on the brink of the Kennedy victory which—through the influence of men like Samuelson—brought Keynesian policies to the country where the conservatism of free capitalism had been most deeply entrenched. The Treaty of Rome was signed in 1957 and the European Economic Community came into being on 1 January 1958. Belgium was a member.

There were plenty of pressures for Belgium to get out of the Congo. The decolonising process had already gone a long way. Asia was now free. Part of Africa was already free; French Africa had received its freedom in 1958; and most of British Africa not already independent was scheduled to become free in the early 1960's. United Nations pressure was increasing. In

1960, the United Nations approved its *Declaration on the Grant-ing of Independence to Colonial Countries and Peoples.*

Suddenly, the Belgian Government decided to give independence to her Congo colony from 1 July 1960. The result, for the Congo, was chaos for a large part of the following decade. It also meant loss for some Belgians who had had employment or interests there and, for a few, it brought death in the sporadic fighting which followed in the years after independence.

But Belgium, as a nation, as a national economy, did not suffer. Not at all. She went from strength to strength. Belgians, who had gone out to the Congo before independence, came home. Many who would have gone stayed to give added strength to the Belgian economy. Capital which would have gone to the Congo, stayed at home. Not all of it. But most of it. The pallor disappeared from the face of the sick man of Europe. His cheeks became healthily pink. As the years passed, he became more and more robust. Belgium's population had been almost static for fifty years. Now, her population began to edge forward. Immigrants began to come from southern Europe. The demand for labour increased so much—and the immigrant labour itself created such a further demand for labour—that the Belgian Government began actively to seek immigrants in southern Europe. From being a country of small emigration, Belgium became a country of significant immigration. From being a country which exported capital, Belgium became a country which also imported so much capital that her status as a net importer or net exporter was pretty much a matter of chance from year to year. From being a country which sought markets everywhere in the world and which worried about a decline in the demand for her sheet glass in Australia or Argentina or Afghanistan, Belgium became a country which had no real need of markets outside Western Europe and North America. There were years in which its exports to her five partners in the European Economic Community increased by more than the whole of her trade with Asia, Africa, Latin America, Oceania and Eastern Europe combined. If, as Belgian Trade Ministers often said, there were good markets going begging in Latin America, that was something which Belgian manufacturers and exporters could acknowledge, but about which they showed little active concern: there were too many other markets, larger and more reliable and closer at hand.

This sensational change was not solely due to Belgium's loss of her colonies. Many factors entered into her new situation of the 1960's. But the loss of the colonies harmonised with this new situation and helped to consolidate it. If Belgian experience is a guide, the great humanitarian movement for decolonisation looks like a clever confidence trick whereby the colonially oppressed have demanded of the colonial powers that the latter do, not what was good for the oppressed, but what was good for the oppressors whose rush to affluence was being retarded by the burdens of an obsolete colonial system. However, the Western European colonial powers were not as clever as this; it is only that, in retrospect, they seem so.

Anyway, as we have already said, it would be wrong to credit decolonisation alone with the marked improvement in the economic situation of the ex-colonial powers after loss of their colonies. Other factors may have been present, and in fact were present, in each case, which must have contributed to the dynamism displayed subsequently. The creation of the European Economic Community from 1st January 1958, was an important element in the economic dynamism of France, the Netherlands and Belgium during the sixties; and the more stable political conditions under the Fifth Republic must have been an additional important element contributing to economic welfare and progress in France after 1958. Certainly, it would be difficult, if not impossible, to quantify any economic benefit which metropolitan countries have derived from loss of their colonies. What can be said is that, on the basis of empirical evidence, loss of colonies caused no grave economic distress to the ex-colonial powers and the evidence leads us to believe that the loss may have been positively and significantly beneficial.

This hypothesis is further supported by the experience of the country which, as decolonisation gathered momentum, took over more and more of the colonial responsibilities, without the direct political control formerly exercised by the colonial powers. Before about 1961—and even as late as 1964, although unemployment was moving fairly steadily downwards then—the United States, compared with other countries in the Western World, battled with recurrent recession, mild compared with pre-war depressions but involving for long periods rates of unemployment between 5 and 7 per cent and considerable unused industrial capacity.

The reasons for the indifferent dynamism of the United States were mainly two, and one operated to reinforce the other. The first cause was United States budgetary and monetary orthodoxy, deriving from a habit of mind and of principle which conditioned the Administration and the Congress to achieve a balanced budget and stable money wherever possible. Often this was not possible and large deficits occurred; but, when it was possible, the budget was balanced whether or not this might have been desirable in the light of the economic growth and employment situation. This remained true despite the long experience of Roosevelt New Deal deficits during the thirties and even though the attitude outside the United States and the attitude of many economists and other individuals within the United States towards fiscal and financial policies, as well as the inbuilt mechanisms to maintain economic stability, had changed a great deal since the Great Depression of 1929 to 1932.

The other main cause of the indifferent dynamism in the United States was the outflow of American funds. Before 1960, net outflow averaged about $5000 million a year. About $3000 million of this in the later years was private investment directed mainly, although not entirely, to highly-developed countries. The remainder consisted of net government grants and capital aid of various kinds to developing countries, and varied from more than $6 billion to about $2 billion a year. Sometimes the percentage of this aid spent on non-American goods and services was very high; at other times, it was claimed that 75 per cent of aid had been tied, formally or in practice, to American goods and services. Even if this latter claim is true, the effect of aid on the dynamism of the American economy during the forties and fifties must have been significant.

The important thing was not that 75 per cent of aid was spent on American goods and services but that 25 per cent was not. If annual aid were $5000 million, this meant that $1250 million was spent on someone else's goods and services. In other words, $1250 million was taken out of the American taxpayers' pocket and neutralised so far as the American economy was concerned. The effect was the same as running a budget surplus of $1250 million a year. If the budget were otherwise balanced, expenditure on foreign aid would give the budget the character of a surplus of this magnitude. If the budget showed a nominal deficit, that deficit would have to equal $1250 million before the adverse impact of foreign aid on the domestic economy was compensated. If the budget showed a nominal surplus, that surplus would have to be increased by the amount of aid spent on foreign goods and services to make a true calculation of the surplus.

This impact on the American economy was largely a result of the United States taking over the responsibility for economic support of the former colonies. Successive United States Presidents 'were guardians of an informal empire of dependencies and client states';[4] but the American responsibility went much further than this. As the colonial powers granted independence, the tendency was for their economic support to decline or not to increase,[5] at least in terms of the real burden, while it became the signal for the commitment of new and sometimes huge funds by the United States for economic, technical and sometimes defence aid. The colonial power which had divested herself of colonial burdens increased her chances of moving forward to full employment, high growth rates and 'economic miracles' with gold at the end of the rainbow and rainbows everywhere astonishingly within reach. The United States on the other hand proceeded, during the forties and fifties, at a level of employment and growth well below the maximum and seemed almost always threatened with a recession of greater or lesser severity.

Nevertheless, up until about 1961, there was a certain balance in the United States situation, although even by then it had been eroded through the recovery from war-damage of the other highly

---

[4] Review of Ronald Steel's 'The Lost Crusade', *New York Times Book Review*, 8 November 1970, p. 38
[5] The record varied for individual colonial powers and individual colonies. *Total* British official aid dropped from $US457 million (0.59% of GNP) in 1961 to $US431 million (0.39% of GNP) in 1969—a very large reduction in real terms. *Total* French aid moved down markedly in real terms and as a percentage of GNP and, after falling by 20 to 25% even in monetary terms, recovered at the end of the 1960's to about the same monetary level as at the beginning of the decade.

developed countries, with a consequent trade challenge which reduced the huge United States trade surplus of the early post-war years. The balance was achieved by this exceptional trade surplus, plus the operation of the United States economy at a level markedly below full employment. The level of operation of the economy varied over time, sometimes threatening levels of employment almost comparable with the thirties (but *not* with the depths of the 1929-32 depression) and at other times promising levels of employment approaching those in Keynesian-type economies. But, since the United States economy operated at a level lower than most other highly developed economies, it tended to run a balance-of-payments surplus which could accommodate the considerable outflow of economic and defence aid and private capital which was, in some ways, analogous to the burdens formerly shouldered by the colonial powers.

In the forties and fifties, there was this balance. In the later fifties, it began to be upset. United States payments surpluses began to be squeezed in two ways. First, foreign trade continued to move back to a more normal pattern and trade surpluses consequently were reduced. Second, bilateral and multilateral aid programmes and expenditures under external defence arrangements, plus the outflow of private capital, not only to the developing countries but also and in particular to Western Europe, tended to increase steadily. The end of the Marshall Plan in Europe did not mean an end to the outflow of American aid but only a beginning or an expansion of aid to the developing countries. The composition of the outflow of United States funds changed but the aggregate demands for unrequited exports and unrequited dollar expenditures steadily increased.

In the late fifties, perhaps it could still be said that there was balance in the United States external position. Or, in any event, such a balance was a prospect. By the early sixties, that had changed. Balance had disappeared. Moreover, there was no real prospect that the balance would be restored. Or no prospect at least unless the United States Government was able and willing to introduce fundamental changes into its political and economic policies. From being a chronic creditor, the United States had quite suddenly become a chronic debtor (although a 'debtor' in a very special sense). She had been a chronic creditor of such magnitude for so long—and her international reserves were so massive—that her status as a chronic debtor did not seem to be clearly recognised for a while and its implications have taken longer to assess.

Perhaps this chronic debtor status would have come anyway, for reasons which we have adumbrated above. But what made it certain, quicker, more continuing and more difficult to control was the adoption of Keynesian policies by the United States Government after the accession of John F. Kennedy to the Presidency in January 1961. By adopting these policies, Kennedy brought the United States up to date. But he also brought the United States into the same sort of economic situation—or his Keynesian policies would shortly bring his country into the same sort of situation—as that which had already compelled or would compel colonial powers to withdraw from their colonial responsibilities. The game was up. The demands of the domestic United States economy would henceforth be too great to allow the outpouring of funds or the adoption of a world role on the scale to which the United States—and the developing countries, as well as United States allies—had become accustomed. From that point, these outlays were destined to run down. They were not, in fact, drastically run down until later in the sixties and then only with some qualifications because earlier attitudes and policies and programmes had caught the United States in commitments which she could not avoid. It was only at the end of the decade that it was clear that 'colonialism'[6] for the United States had ended or was ending just as it had ended for most of the colonial powers before it.

All of the above generalises some broad, empirical evidence. For the most part, the evidence is made to show that countries practising Keynesian policies and attempting at the same time to accept colonial responsibilities and burdens are likely to go broke. It attempts to show this on the basis that countries which have given up colonial burdens have been solvent afterwards; countries which have contrived to shoulder colonial burdens—

---

[6] 'Colonialism' is not used here in any pejorative way. It is applied to the United States only in the sense that she assumed many of the economic and defence burdens which, in an earlier period, had been assumed by the colonial powers. She exercised none of the direct political and military control which had been characteristic of colonial rule.

even though reducing them or changing their form—have continued to risk insolvency; and the country which above all has taken over colonial burdens has—especially since its concurrent application of Keynesian policies—constantly courted insolvency. There is a large element of *post-hoc-ergo-propter-hoc* reasoning in all this: because one thing follows another in time, therefore the first is assumed to be the cause of the second.

A lot more surrounding evidence is therefore needed to show that the conclusions drawn from the broad empirical evidence are valid. The conclusions are no more than hypotheses. These hypotheses may not bear more searching examination. But if other surrounding and convincing evidence can be adduced to show that they are true—and we believe that it can—then this will be of great significance to the relations between developed and developing countries and to the latters' future economic progress. To put it at the level of the least significance, it is one thing for aid and export of capital—with the accompanying temporary migration of personnel—to be of no or negligible benefit to the donor country. This sort of neutral situation is one which most developed countries might be prepared to tolerate; in fact, it would, to many people and governments, seem to have the advantage of being more 'moral' than a situation in which the donor country won some 'imperialist' or 'capitalist' or 'exploitative' benefit from its capital and management involvement in a developing country. But, while this might be acceptable, it is quite another and much more serious matter if the provision of economic and technical aid and the investment of private capital in developing countries threaten economic growth and employment at home. Full employment and a rapidly rising GNP have increasingly become the preoccupations of governments everywhere. They are gods which must be assuaged. Anyone or anything which stands in their way must be swept aside.

If it is the developing countries which are standing in the way, then they must be allowed to do it no longer. And there are few people who would say that that refusal was unreasonable. The result may be to divide the world into two groups of the 'haves' and the 'havenots'—the 'big' countries and the 'peripheral' countries—even more sharply in the future than at present.

VII
A World Divided

We already have an economically divided world. If what we have already said and what we yet have to say are valid, the world is going to be much more divided still. There is both theoretical and empirical evidence leading to this conclusion.

Let us summarize some of the points already made.

The Keynesian economy is a full employment economy. It is a high growth economy. It is an economy of affluent consumers. Its domestic market is large, stable and sophisticated. Tertiary industries tend to be more important than either primary or secondary industries and to be growing steadily more important. The growth of service industries tends to complete the concentration of population which the earlier growth of secondary industry had commenced.

The economy turns inward. Except in certain ways. Those ways include exchange of industrial goods with other developed economies. The developed economies tend—with a lot of uglifying warts and spots—to become a single, large, industrial market. This market reaches out to draw supplies of food and raw materials from wherever they are most cheaply available. Capital flows are concentrated within each developed economy and among the developed economies.

Gradually the great industrial, service and capital economies become more and more integrated. Barriers to industrial goods are gradually removed. Barriers to primary goods aren't.

And they aren't between the developed and the developing countries either. But the developed countries—the 'big' countries—buy the food and raw materials they need beyond their own domestic production from the developing countries—the 'peripheral' countries. The latter are peripheral because they are not, except as suppliers of food and raw materials, vital to the economic well-being of the 'big' countries. And food and raw materials—up until now, in any event—can be got from many sources, any time;[1] for those commodities, it is not quite, but nearly always a buyer's, not a seller's market.

So there tend to be two groups of countries: one group preoccupied with their own ever-increasing economic growth, dynamism and affluence; the other group preoccupied with their relations with the first group and eternally aspiring to the economic growth, dynamism and affluence which the first group enjoys.

Something of this situation can be conveyed by a few sets of statistics. Let's have a look at some of them.

First, how much of the world's trade is done by the developed countries and how much by the developing countries?

The two accompanying tables show how relatively small the trade of developing market economies is. Moreover, the tendency over the last twenty years has been for the trade of these economies to decline both as a percentage of world trade and as a percentage of the trade of the developed market economies. In 1938, the trade of the developing market economies was 23.9 per cent of total world trade and 35.5 per cent of the trade of the developed market economies. By 1948, when the more advanced economies were still suffering from the devastation of the Second World War, these percentages had risen to 29.5 per cent and 45.8 per cent respectively. But that was about the high point. By 1959, the percentages—at 22.4 and 34.3 respectively—were already down below the 1938 level; and by 1968, they had slipped well below this level to 18.3 per cent of world trade and 25.9 per

[1] The recent solidarity of OPEC (the major oil-producing countries) in forcing up the price for oil to the consuming countries might presage similar concerted action by exporters of other primary products. But oil is a commodity which offers greater opportunities for pressure by producers than most, if not all, others. Therefore, it may not in practice furnish the precedent which it suggests in theory.

cent of the trade of the developed market economies. The prospect is that this trend will persist, that there will be a much sharper growth in the trade of the developed countries and that the trade of developing countries will continue to lose significance, in relation both to developed market economies' trade and world trade as a whole. The trade of developing countries is still large in aggregate terms but, as we have discussed already elsewhere, the components of this trade, its stability and its dynamism compared with that of the developed countries make it less significant than statistical aggregates would make it appear.

TRADE OF DEVELOPED MARKET ECONOMIES AND DEVELOPING MARKET ECONOMIES
1938 to 1968: and 1948 to 1968

	Imports	Exports	Total Trade	Imports	Exports	Total Trade
	1938 (*$US billions*)			1968 (*$US billions*)		
Developed Market Economies	17.9	15.2	33.1	178.6	168.1	346.7
Developing Market Economies	5.8	5.9	11.7	45.8	44.1	89.9
	1948 (*$US billions*)			1968 (*$US billions*)		
Developed Market Economies	41.2	36.7	77.9	178.6	168.1	346.7
Developing Market Economies	18.6	17.1	35.7	45.8	44.1	89.9

DEVELOPING MARKET ECONOMIES' TRADE AS A PERCENTAGE OF WORLD TRADE AND AS A PERCENTAGE OF DEVELOPED MARKET ECONOMIES' TRADE
1938 to 1968

Year	As a Percentage of World Trade	As a Percentage of Developed Market Economies' Trade
	%	%
1938	23.9	35.9
1948	29.5	45.8
1959	22.4	34.3
1968	18.3	25.9

On 30 October 1970, Professor Paul A. Samuelson wrote that the question he was most often asked when lecturing abroad was 'Doesn't America's prosperity depend upon Cold War expenditures and imperialistic ventures like that in Viet-Nam?' He said that the reply he gave was, 'When Lenin and Rosa Luxembourg advanced the thesis of capitalism's dependence on outside markets for its prosperity, William Howard Taft was President and Maynard Keynes still a dilettante undergraduate at Cambridge. In the old-fashioned *laissez-faire* economy, prosperity was indeed a fragile blossom. But for a modern "mixed economy" in the post-Keynesian era, fiscal and monetary policies can definitely prevent chronic slumps, can offset automation or under-consumption, can insure that resources find paying work opportunities. The two fastest-growing mixed economies have been Germany and Japan —both stripped of their colonies and forbidden to have armies— which is empirical proof of Keynes's theoretical refutation of the imperialism thesis.'

The statistics we have given above, if not empirical proof, certainly supply some empirical evidence of the relative slightness of the dependence of the developed countries on markets in the developing countries.

We can take other figures which strengthen this empirical evidence in the direction of empirical proof. For example, the following tables show the trade of some major developed countries, including the European Economic Community, with the rest of the world and with the developed and the developing market economies in 1957 and 1968. In the case of Britain, exports to the developing economies scarcely increased at all, even in monetary terms, over the eleven-year period, while United States exports to these economies increased by about 25 per cent in monetary terms. On the other hand, British and American exports to the developed market economies almost doubled over the eleven-year period. The story was, in one respect, less sensational for the European Economic Community, in that exports to the developing market economies increased by about 50 per cent. However, in another respect the EEC figures were even more sensational, for exports to the developed market economies more than trebled, from $16.2 billion in 1957 to $51.8 billion in 1968. Japan's dependence on developing countries, especially in Asia,

remained much more a factor in her trade; but, even so, a fundamental change had taken place. In 1957, Japan exported about
half as much again—$1.7 billion—to developing market economies
as she exported—$1.1 billion—to developed market economies.
By 1968, the figures had changed to $5.6 billion and $6.8 billion
respectively. Exports to the developing market economies had
grown by $3.9 billion, whereas exports to the developed market
economies had grown by $5.7 billion, to make the latter clearly
the larger and conspicuously the more dynamic of Japan's
markets.

	Total Exports	Total Exports
	1957	1968
	$US billions	
European Economic Community	23.2	64.2
Britain	9.5	14.8
United States	20.7	34.2
Japan	2.9	13.0

	Total Exports to Developing Market Economies		Total Exports to Developed Market Economies	
	1957	1968	1957	1968
	$US billions			
European Economic Community	6.1	9.3	16.2	51.8
Britain	3.4	3.6	5.9	10.7
United States	8.0	10.7	12.5	23.3
Japan	1.7	5.6	1.1	6.8

These figures might seem to carry some implication that those
countries which have increased their trade most with the developing countries have been more dynamic than those countries which
have succeeded less in these markets; and that consequently their
dynamism is related to their trade with developing economies.
A more reasonable implication is that their dynamism is related to
their capacity to increase their total exports, an increasing abso-

lute amount and proportion of which have gone to developed economies.

What is happening therefore is that the world economy is separating more and more into two groups. Apart from the distinctive characteristics we have already noted, the first group consists of those countries among whom the traditional, tough commercial negotiation of the past is still possible and practical; offers and demands can be put and balanced and a decent bargain struck. If Britain wants to join the European Economic Community, she can negotiate her way in. There can be political complications of the kind which resulted in France placing a veto on British entry to bring an end to the 1961 to 1963 negotiations. But the basis is there for a deal. In the negotiations which began in 1970, Britain can achieve membership if she is willing to accept the Treaty of Rome and make the policy adjustments according to a time schedule which the present members of the EEC require. Similarly, during the series of tariff negotiations which have taken place under the General Agreement on Tariffs and Trade—the latest of which was the Kennedy Round—it was possible for the developed countries to strike bargains with each other. There was a lot of hard bargaining and, in all the negotiations, the tariff reductions achieved fell short of the results which were aimed at. But a good deal was achieved. Tariffs were reduced over a wide range of industrial goods and the percentage reduction in individual tariffs—especially if we take account of the succession of negotiations, and not a single round—was considerable. Trade in industrial products among the developed countries was generally made much freer. This was one of the reasons for the substantial increase in trade among developed countries in the last twenty years. It was not the fundamental reason for this expansion—indeed, those more fundamental causes were themselves the stimuli for the tariff negotiations—but they were a contributing cause and helped to keep the expansion going and intensifying.

But none of this was true for the second group of countries—the 'peripheral' or developing countries. The trade among the developed countries—the trade of industrial goods for industrial goods—was the dynamic trade. That was the trade worth negotiating for. The developing countries lay outside this trade. Any negotiations in which they might participate as equals or near equals would need to be based on exchange of industrial goods for primary products. All the exports of all the developing countries are not primary products, but most of them are; and they can strike a reasonable bargain in trade negotiations only if the countries they are negotiating with are willing to give concessions on access for primary products against concessions for access for industrial products.

And this the developed countries are not prepared to do. It just does not constitute a commercial bargain for them. Although the needs of the developing countries are great, they are not needs for which they can negotiate effectively with the developed countries. They are not in a position to make commercial offers which are meaningful or reasonable in relation to their commercial requests.

In these circumstances, the international arrangements which have been established for negotiations on economic matters are of virtually no use to the developing countries. They are rich men's clubs. In all those respects which are germane to its original purpose, the General Agreement on Tariffs and Trade is a means of governing trade and adjusting tariffs among the advanced countries.

In the course of time, GATT has been modified to give some attention to the needs of developing countries. This has meant that those developing countries which are Contracting Parties to GATT are, in effect, observers at the tariff and other genuine economic negotiations which take place under GATT; they are active participants and direct beneficiaries of the rules of GATT only when special arrangements are extended, for non-economic reasons, by the developed to the developing countries.

This situation is made more explicit under UNCTAD (the United Nations Conference on Trade and Development). Unlike GATT, which was established shortly after the Second World War to lay down trade rules and to arrange balanced, mutually beneficial trade negotiations among countries who were assumed to be able to bargain with each other more or less as equals, UNCTAD was established much later, in 1964, as a means whereby the strong could make non-reciprocal, unbalanced, one-way concessions to the weak.

It is in UNCTAD that the two groups of developed and un-developed countries are most clear-cut. The developing group of 'seventy-seven' as it is called—although its membership now numbers many more than seventy-seven—tries to work and bargain as a single cohesive unit. The principal group with which it bargains—the 'Western European and Others' group—similarly seeks to achieve a consensus of views and to negotiate as a unit with the 'Seventy-seven'.

While this UNCTAD arrangement tends clearly to confirm the existence of two distinct groups of countries in the world economy, experience within UNCTAD as well as evidence outside it confirms—as one would expect—that there is a whole continuous spectrum of development with clusters of countries at every point in this spectrum. This applies to the developed as well as the developing countries, although the range of diversity in the former tends to be less than in the latter. As with almost any grouping of countries, there are some countries which are clearly in one group and some clearly in the other. The United States is manifestly a developed country; Chad is with equal lack of ambiguity a developing country. But there are also some countries which are at the margin between the two and which appear in some respects and in some contexts to belong to one group and in other respects and contexts to the other. Argentina is included in the 'Seventy-seven' but often feels a greater affinity with the developed countries than with some of her developing fellows, for example, in Africa, which are at the very beginning of the development process. Australia and New Zealand are in the 'Western European and Others' group but have some characteristics which liken them to developing countries. For example, they are both heavily dependent on the export of primary products for overseas earnings and they are both regular net importers of capital.

However, having acknowledged that there is this spectrum of development and that there is this shading of one group into another, it nevertheless remains true that the two groups do exist and that, with the qualifications we have noted, they are identifiable. The developed countries are the 'GATT' countries; the developing countries are the 'UNCTAD' countries.

The GATT countries tend to be high-income industrial-exporting countries; the UNCTAD countries are low-income, primary-commodity-exporting countries. By and large, these distinctions hold good, especially at the extreme ends of the spectrum. The countries of Western Europe are GATT countries and, by and large, they are high-income, industrial-exporting countries. Countries in Africa like Burundi and Nigeria are UNCTAD countries and they are low-income, primary-exporting countries.

There are sometimes qualifications to these criteria for identification. For example, France is a GATT country and a high-income country but, as well as being an industrial exporter, she is also a primary exporter and, having this dual status, she can bargain for those primary exports. So, to some extent, can the United States. A country like Australia is a high-income country whose population is mainly engaged in secondary and tertiary industry but she is essentially a primary-commodity exporter. She belongs wholly neither to the GATT nor to the UNCTAD countries but, in some respects, fulfils the criteria of both.

Allowing for these marginal countries and these overlapping characteristics, we can distinguish the two groups as follows. The first group consists of high-income, highly-industrialised countries with a large population, or integrated in a larger group, which are undergoing or are capable of undergoing a constant dynamic economic growth and therefore providing a ready extension of the domestic market of other countries similarly placed. These include the former colonial powers which have now withdrawn from their colonies and countries which could have been colonial powers in the era of colonialism, and they include also the country or countries which have assumed some of the burdens of the colonial powers in the post-colonial era.

The second group consists of low-income, non-industrialised or modestly industrialised countries which, even though they may have a large population and may have a high growth rate, do not offer any promise of a considerable extension of the domestic market of the highly-industrialised countries for some time to come. Though this group includes some countries which have never been colonies, the group consists mainly of former colonies which have now won their independence or from which the colonial power has now withdrawn.

The first group will continue to conduct mutually advantageous negotiations on economic matters among themselves. They, or significant sub-groups among them, will tend to move in the direction of free trade in industrial products and will tend to create sub-groups for industrial free trade areas or industrial customs unions. They will also tend, as far as circumstances—including their relations with developing countries—allow, to facilitate the free flow of capital among the whole group or among sub-groups of their membership. This free or relatively free flow of industrial products and capital will, to the extent that it is achieved and maintained, add to their already high degree of economic dynamism.

The second group will have little or no negotiating power in a purely commercial or economic sense, and will therefore be forced to hoist themselves to higher levels of living through chance beneficence of the market, through protecting their own domestic market, and through benefits which might come to them incidentally through application of most-favoured-nation rules after negotiations among the first group of countries have lowered tariffs in the developed countries. Alternatively, or additionally, they might obtain benefits for reasons which are not commercial: they might receive technical and economic aid or they might receive such things as preferential tariff treatment for developing countries. But these benefits will be gifts, to be extended somewhat arbitrarily, by the first group of countries. The important thing is that the capacity of the second group of countries to negotiate on economic matters—to sit round a table and bargain as equals or near-equals with the first group of countries—does not exist. This situation is unlikely to be remedied in the foreseeable future but, on the contrary, might become more sharply evident, perhaps for a generation, perhaps longer.

The reasons for this division of the world economy into two groups with an erosion of economic interdependence between them are those given earlier:

1 A rapid rise in the level of consumption of the average consumer in the advanced countries;

2 The achievement of high and steady economic growth in the advanced countries at high levels of human and capital employment;

3 The constantly increasing sophistication of industrial production and consumer services which is both a reflection of and
a stimulus to the constantly more sophisticated consumer in the
advanced countries.

The movement of the modern economy proportionately away
from what might be called material production to production of
services is also an important element in the division of the world
economy and, under present conditions, in the loss of economic
significance and negotiating power by the developing countries.

The increasing importance of service industries has hastened a
trend which has gone on since the beginning of the Industrial
Revolution towards ever greater concentration of population. The
service industries are not the only reason for this concentration.
They are only one of the more recent and dynamic of the elements
which sustain and intensify it. A number of factors combine together to cause what is, as we might say, a 'gold-rush effect' in the
modern economy and in the world economy as a whole. It is to
this gold-rush effect that we shall now turn.

VIII
The Gold-rush Effect

The nineteenth century colonial period was a time in which European industrialists, traders and investors reached everywhere. The rush for markets and the rush for colonies, while not synonymous, had enough in common for the one to reinforce the other. The European countries competed vigorously with one another to gain both more colonies and more markets—a competition which often brought the competitors to the brink of war. But just as the fashion was once to win colonies, so more recently the fashion[1] has been to get out of colonies. Where once the effort was for extensive economic exploitation, now the effort is for more intensive exploitation within limited areas. Where once populations spread themselves—whether as soldiers, traders or settlers—all over the world, now the tendency is for populations of advanced economies to concentrate themselves in highly urbanised areas, with highly specialised services and talents providing much of the centripetal force for further concentration. There is nothing surprising in this relatively sudden turnabout. Change is characteristic of modern economies.

In modern economies, equilibrium is an abnormal economic situation. The norm is movement. Prices, wages, investment, stock-exchange indexes, production, inventories, exports and imports are usually going up or going down; they are static—

[1] Always excepting countries such as Portugal, which have so far remained outside the mainstream of Western European economic progress.

they maintain an unchanging level—for only brief periods. More-over, a movement in a certain direction tends to be cumulative; if share prices begin to move up, the movement in itself creates an expectation of further rises which prompts them to rise still more; an increase in employment tends to have a multiplier effect on the demand both for labour and commodities, so that further increases in employment are probable; a net emigration of people from an area creates conditions which make it probable that more people will move out at an increasing rate, and so emigration causes an accelerating loss of population; while the country of immigration experiences an accelerating gain.

This tendency has been observable on a regional, national and world scale since the end of the War. Movement of people has in itself created conditions for further movement. Movement of capital has created incentives for further movement along the same route. Concentration of economic activity in one area has increased the advantages of further concentration in that same area. Some movements are temporary; the upward movement of one element is accompanied or followed shortly afterwards by the downward movement of another, or vice versa, with the one eventually offsetting the other. In other cases, the movement seems to be permanent—or likely to operate as far ahead as one can see—and several movements seem to operate in the same direction simultaneously.

Let us take a few examples. In the years after 1945, there was a massive movement of refugees out of East Germany into West Germany. The East German economy lacked vigour, production fell, farms were abandoned or had inadequate labour and even industrial production failed to show strength and vigour. As this happened, the stimuli to further large-scale emigration of East Germans to the West were intensified and this emigration in itself further worsened the situation which had called it forth. Although there must be some ultimately inhibiting factors—or else perhaps Ireland, for example, would have been completely depopulated in the nineteenth century—the worst nightmares of Ulbricht's East German regime must have included the vision that the whole East German population would eventually disappear across the Western borders. After strenuous efforts to stop refugee move-ment by other means, the East German regime ultimately took the politically damning step of building a wall in East Berlin and policing it ruthlessly to keep the East German population at home. Since then, though there has been widespread revulsion at the draconian inhumanity of making a prison for millions of people and although morale in East Germany may still not be high, there has been a stabilising of the population and a considerable improvement in the vigour and growth of the economy.

West Germany, on the other hand, was the destination of these East German (and other) refugees. About 2 million East Germans reached the West during the fifties. Some of them went on to other destinations outside Europe. But most of them stayed in West Germany. They came in such numbers that absorption, in the early years, was difficult and comparatively slow. As time passed and the West German Wirtschaftswunder got under way, their absorption became much easier. The refugees themselves contributed to the 'economic miracle' because they were a ready source of labour and they were a vigorous source of demand to stimulate and continue the boom. But another element contributed to the economic miracle: the flood of United States aid to Germany. The two elements—available capital and available labour—brought Germany very quickly out of the chaos of the post-war period. As the flow of refugees from East Germany diminished and then virtually stopped, its place was partially taken by a flow of labour from such countries in southern Europe as Italy, Spain, Yugoslavia and Turkey. The southern European communities in Germany are now large and easily discernible even to the casual tourist. They became an important element in Germany's continued economic growth.

The flow of American capital to Germany never completely stopped. Its form changed. Instead of being Governmental aid, it became private investment. The boom in Germany and the relative recession in the United States, in many years and over a long period, maintained the private investment flow and that, in turn, tended to sustain both the German boom and the tendency to United States recession. The additional dynamism apparently deriving from the development of the European Economic Community, the possible permanence given to this dynamism by the Community, and the desire of United States firms to get inside the huge free market foreshadowed by the EEC helped not only to sustain but to increase the flow of United States investment funds to Germany. This in turn gave increased vigour to the German economy and increased the need to import additional labour from southern Europe; and this vigour was not diminished by unrequited outlays on the scale which has plagued the United States and Britain in their performance of a 'world role'. There has thus been a constant interaction between various elements tending to lead the German economy on to ever higher levels of activity.

One commentator towards the end of 1970 wrote that, 'on the surface, the German economy in 1970 still seems a paradise to most outside observers. Who else has kept up a growth rate of 5 per cent this year, with consumer prices rising at only 4 per cent? Who else has managed to combine this with an unemployment figure of below 100,000 (or well under 1 per cent of the labour force) but with over 800,000 vacancies and two million guest workers. Despite last year's upvaluation, Germany has enjoyed a nice little current account surplus on its external payments as well.'[2] An accompanying chart (see below) showed that, in about four years, earnings per employee had gone up by about 35 per cent, while consumer prices had gone up by only 11 per cent.

The surprising thing was that this commentator showed surprise. Given the elements in the German situation, the results were what might have been expected. To extract only one element, the commentator implied surprise that the German economy could accommodate 'two million guest workers' and still achieve all those other splendid things. But the 'two million guest workers' were in fact one of the things which *enabled* the German economy to achieve what it did. The commentator suggested—and this was the reason that he used the phrase 'on the surface' to qualify his glowing description of the German economy—that the German authorities might have to 'tighten their present credit squeeze, to try to cause a little more unemployment and bring wage demands back to a lower level'.[3] If, in fact, the German authorities were to do this, then the German mystique could, in our view, well be shattered, and the German

[2] *The Economist*, 7-13 November 1970, p. 69
[3] Ibid., p. 70

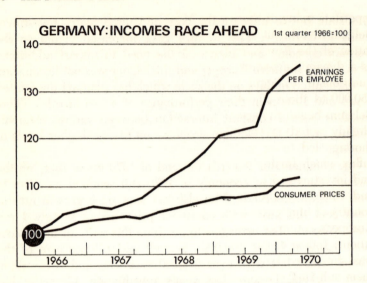

Source: *The Economist,* 7-13 November 1970

economy might get on the same slippery slide as other economies before it. Germany would still have certain advantages—including relatively small unrequited external outlays—but she would not need to play too fast and loose with her blessings if she were to maintain her present enviable internal and external equilibrium.

As this analysis implies, there is nothing—or very little— uniquely German in the recent German economic experience. Details have differed, but the experience of all the member countries of the European Economic Community has been, in essence, much the same when they have shared the elements which have given the German economy its strength. In Belgium, a small country, the boom came late and was largely the creation of the boom conditions intensifying in the two large neighbouring countries of France and Germany. The boom in France, after 1958, set alongside the vigorous and constantly mounting expansion of Germany, almost coincided with independence for the Belgian Congo in 1960, which tended to reduce the outward movement of Belgian nationals and capital to the Congo, to repatriate many of those who had been there and to concentrate Belgian investment at home. It also coincided with the inauguration of the European Economic Community whose character as a dynamic economic influence seemed, after 1960, to be unquestioned. Unemployment in Belgium dropped from about 150,000 to about 40,000 in the course of three or four years and Belgium began to experience an acute labour shortage of a kind already noted in some other Western countries. This labour shortage led to an influx of labour from Southern Europe, an influx which further accentuated the boom both in employment and investment. From being a country with a stable population and a mild tendency to emigration, Belgium became, by 1964, a country of immigration, with offices established in some Southern European countries, including Italy and Spain, to recruit migrant labour. Inflow of capital, from the United States and elsewhere, was stimulated by these developments and, in turn, stimulated them still further.

The same situation occurred in Holland and France: buoyant economic conditions attracted labour from the south and the migrant labour in turn accentuated both the demand for labour and the incentives for investment. Rates of economic growth tended to increase. In Italy, the movement of labour was largely internal. The sort of economic dynamism experienced in Germany, France, Belgium and Holland tended, in Italy, to be regionally concentrated in the north. The south, which was not well-placed to share the industrial boom with the north, had large reserves of labour which had traditionally moved either north or overseas. Now the movement to northern Italy was accelerated; differences between north and south in terms of concentration of population and industry tended to be accentuated; and the north, whose vigour had stimulated the movement in the first instance, fed on the movement to enhance its own dynamism from the forces which it had itself set in motion.

No one would suggest that the circumstances in all these countries were identical. They were not. But vital elements were common to them all. Some of these same elements were also present even in Britain, which, with all its cross-Channel differences, was nevertheless caught up in something of the same process. Britain achieved a high level of employment and (with important qualifications) economic activity almost constantly since the end of the War. During this period, there was a considerble inflow of capital into the country, especially from the United States and Europe. But there was also a simultaneous outflow of investment capital from Britain, especially since 1954. In the decade 1954-64, British investments overseas increased from £stg.4000 million to £stg.11,000 million. Whether there was a net inflow or outflow of capital during this period is hard to say, but it seems reasonable to hazard a guess that inflow must have balanced much of the outflow, for otherwise the disequilibrium in Britain's external payments would have compelled even more drastic measures much earlier to restore a payments equilibrium. Among these measures—and leaving aside policies of deflation which would have been politically quite unacceptable at the intensity which would have been needed to restore equilibrium— would have been sharp cutbacks in private capital outflow, in governmental economic aid, and in defence spending especially overseas, and perhaps a much more urgent programme of de-colonisation.

Not only has Britain experienced a two-way flow of capital since the Second World War, but she has also experienced a two-way flow of migrants.

The traditional British emigration to Canada, the United States, Australia, New Zealand and so on persisted after the Second World War, although fluctuations in the rate were considerable and there were periodic changes in the destination most favoured by British emigrants. Without any compensating inward flow, this emigration reduced the rate of increase in the British popu-lation, tended to make the British economy overcapitalised, reduced the rate of growth of the gross national product and produced for Britain generally something of the same problems —although not in the same measure—as those experienced at one time or another by Ireland, Greece or East Germany. The extent of these problems was in any event reduced, for a period, by a considerable inflow of migrants of Commonwealth or foreign stock which compensated for the outflow of migrants of British stock (see attached table). Britain, with a long tradition of free immigration, especially from the Commonwealth, attracted large numbers of people not only from the dominions of British stock

but from countries with predominantly Asian or African populations. These people were attracted by the boom conditions in
Britain, by the easy employment opportunities and by the high
wage-levels compared with those in their home countries.
Britain offered them an opportunity for a much richer material
life than was offering to them at home, even though the standards which they were prepared to accept were below those
of the indigenous Briton. In turn, the labour which they had to
offer was welcome to the British economy; plentiful employment
at high wages had made it extremely difficult to fill jobs at the
lower, unskilled levels of the economy; and these were just the
jobs which the non-European immigrants from the Commonwealth were prepared to fill.

There was therefore a harmony between supply and demand
which made movement almost inevitable provided no governmental restrictions were placed in its way. Moreover it was not
a movement which tended, in economic terms, to remove the
causes which called it forth. On the contrary, the influx of
immigrants helped to sustain and intensify the boom in Britain
and to create further employment opportunities for further groups
of non-European immigrants. The flow therefore tended to be a
constantly increasing one which only a sharp downturn in the
economy, approximating to a pre-war depression rather than a
post-war recession, would have brought to a halt for economic
reasons.

Over the eighteen-year period from 1950 to 1968, real gross
domestic product, both in total and per capita terms, increased
at its greatest rate between 1960 and 1965.[4] So also did real gross
domestic product in agriculture, in manufacturing, in total
industrial activity, in construction, in transport and communications. Private consumption expenditure, general government
consumption expenditure and gross domestic fixed capital formation also increased at their greatest rate between 1960 and 1965.
Even the British balance of payments (see attached table
showing Britain's international reserves) was seldom healthier
than when the immigrants were flooding in. The average reserves

---

[4] That is, of the six-year periods 1950-55, 1955-60, 1960-65 and the
shorter period 1965-68. If figures were available for 1958 to 1963, this
would almost certainly be even better than 1960-65.

when there was a net inflow of migrants from 1958 to 1963 were $US3233 million. The average for the preceding three years (1955 to 1957) was only $US2347 million, and for the following five years (1964 to 1968) only $2707 million. There are obviously a mass of factors affecting the balance-of-payments and reserves position of any country; but it would be an interesting study to see how far the reversal of the usual migration flow between 1958 and 1963 affected Britain's external financial position.

BRITAIN: MIGRATION AND INTERNATIONAL RESERVES
1953 to 1967

Year	Net Migration	International Monetary Reserves*
1953	− 74,000	
1954	− 32,000	
1955	− 10,000	2392
1956	− 17,000	2276
1957	− 72,000	2374
1958	+ 45,000	3105
1959	+ 44,000	2801
1960	+ 82,000	3719
1961	+170,000	3318
1962	+136,000	3308
1963	+ 10,000	3147
1964	− 59,300	2316
1965	− 77,600	3004
1966	− 81,900	3100
1967	− 85,900	2695
1968		2422

Net Migration 1955-1960 inclusive:	+ 12,000
Net Migration 1960-1965 inclusive:	+ 43,500
Average international reserves 1955-57:	$US 2347 million
Average international reserves 1958-63:	$US 3233 million
Average international reserves 1964-68:	$US 2707 million

* Gold Holdings + Reserve position in the International Monetary Fund + Foreign Exchange.

For these economic reasons, it would have been advantageous to both Britain and the countries providing the migrants if the flow had continued and perhaps continued at an accelerating rate, subject only to the capacity of the British economy to absorb them (in terms of accommodation, services and so on) before reaching some point—and that point needs a good deal of refinement of definition—at which intolerable inflationary strains might have appeared. The element which compelled a restriction on the flow of immigrants was not economic but social. The influx of large numbers of people accustomed to and prepared to accept lower standards of living—and identifiable as groups whose continued entry into the society could be limited or prohibited—created conditions of social conflict which compelled the British Government to place restraints on the immigrant flow even though it was beneficial to the economy. Then the gold-rush effect in the United Kingdom was reversed. Immigration was reduced below levels which it would otherwise have attained and emigration was not only maintained but was given an added stimulus through the check to growth caused by the restriction of immigration. The gold-rush effect of immigration into Britain was thus converted into a reverse gold-rush effect of emigration from Britain. Paradoxically perhaps, hostility against the immigrant groups grew when restrictions had been imposed against their further entry and when these restrictions contributed to a downturn in British economic fortunes.

What the gold-rush effect means is that powerful economic forces tend to concentrate population more and more in particular locations. Labour moves to these locations and investment which preceded the movement of that labour and which inspired it, expands still more to accommodate them and their families and their successors. Housing has to be provided for their shelter. Retail shops are needed to sell them food and clothing. Schools are needed for their children. Doctors and hospitals are needed to look after their health. And there is a whole range of people from plumbers to musicians, bankers to dance instructors, needed to provide them with services.

Big concentrations of population are better able to provide the range and excellence of skills, as well as the quantity of labour, required by large industrial and commercial organisations. They are better able to provide professional, industrial, commercial services and banking, educational and cultural services.

Modern concentrations of populations are less related to the location of natural resources than in the past. Population doesn't concentrate on good farming land or on coalfields or even necessarily round steel mills. Locations must enjoy certain advantages if they are to be suitable for large concentrations of populations.

They need good sea, land and/or air communications and they need, for example, plentiful supplies of water. But the things they must have are relatively few.

What is absolutely essential, however, is that, for some reason or another, people should have already concentrated at a particular location and/or that there is a powerful stimulus for them to concentrate there in the future. So long as that can be maintained, the flow will continue unabated in present economic circumstances, and cities will grow into sprawling collections of urban aggregations almost *ad infinitum.*

Population from Scotland and Ireland, from Wales, and from the north and west of England moves down into the south-east corner of England, especially around London. As London gains population, its discomforts grow but so does its dynamism. The areas from which the population departs often become a paradise of tranquillity for the visitor but they also become more and more economically depressed, over-capitalised and tending to chronic economic stagnation. The government develops plans for decentralisation and regional development and desperately struggles to reverse economic forces, not because of their economic effects, but because they carry with them unacceptable social and political results. 'In nearly 3000 miles of driving our rental car from Perth to John o'Groats's House, on the north-eastern tip of Scotland, with many a side trip', a returnee[5] to his Scottish homeland wrote with nostalgic delight after three decades absence, 'I saw hardly a bill-board, met another car only every ten minutes or so, and drank happily from gurgling mountain burns, cold and clean as the stones of the Cairngorm Mountains. The Scots have not yet learned to pollute themselves.' The pollution is where the progress is. Even the tourists going to Scotland stick mainly to Edinburgh and the finest economic prospect a Scot ever sees is still the high road that leads him to London and south-east England—or to New York or Sydney or Toronto.

Much the same population movements have occurred elsewhere. In France, population has moved out of the rural areas and, generally, from the south and west to the north and east. In Belgium, population has concentrated around Brussels-

[5] Ian Glass in *The New York Times,* 22 November 1970

Antwerp. In Germany, it has moved again out of rural areas to concentrate in the Ruhr-Rhine valley and along the North Sea Coast. In Italy, population has moved especially from the south up to the industrial areas of the north. Outside Europe, in some of the less highly developed of the developed countries, the same process is already under way. For example, population in Australia has increasingly concentrated in the two major urban agglomerations of Sydney and Melbourne, which together contain about 40 per cent of the total Australian population.

The flow of population is therefore to the large population centres. Within a country, this is so. Internationally, it tends to be true also. Movement internationally tends to be related to incentives to movement within the national economy and vice versa. When economic conditions within Italy were depressed, there tended to be a large-scale movement of Italian migrants to the United States, Canada, Australia, and other countries in Western Europe. There was some internal migration too, especially from the south to the industrial areas of the north but, so long as the Italian economy was depressed, say, in the 1940's and 1950's, this movement was less and the movement to foreign destinations more than in later years. After 1960, associated especially with the boom conditions which followed the formation of the European Common Market, Italy entered a period of high employment—or relatively high compared with the earlier post-war years—high investment and high economic growth. The concentration of population in the industrial centres increased; urban agglomerations expanded. Foreign emigration continued but at a declining rate.

The same thing happened in other European countries as better economic conditions developed. Fewer Greeks and Irish went abroad and in Ireland, for about the first time in more than a century, emigration fell below natural increase and the population started to grow. Just as in East Germany, the slowing down and then the elimination of population loss improved economic conditions still further; it provided a further incentive for labour and capital to remain in the domestic economy and enticed more capital from abroad.

The process once under way, it will continue until some new elements bring it to a halt. In conditions of free movement of labour and capital, labour will, after a certain stage has been reached, move in from any outside source from which it is available: into Belgium and Germany from Spain, Greece, Turkey, Italy and Yugoslavia; into Britain from the Commonwealth, including India, Pakistan and the West Indies. The continuing inflow of population will stimulate further investment, especially in housing, educational and health facilities and services, as well as in establishments for the supply of more consumer goods, including consumer durables. The economy receiving the new population will become more and more preoccupied with itself and less and less concerned with the external world. Emigration will decline and might, to all intents and purposes, disappear. The same will happen to the export of capital. The effect on exports may be uncertain but the increased supply of labour will be one factor tending to increase the output of export industries and perhaps reducing the need for imports. The net immigration will tend to be predominantly of people of working age with, in some cases, young dependants. People of working age will tend to be a higher proportion of the immigrant group than in the receiving community as a whole. Benefit flows from benefit.

Here is the gold-rush effect going on and ever on: its main characteristics are increasing population, increasing urbanisation, growing investment and more intensive preoccupation with the home economy. But instead of going on and on, it can be stopped and reversed. If the inflow of migrants causes social problems which compel its restriction or limitation, if domestic or external policies cause inflationary or balance-of-payments difficulties which force—so it is now thought—the adoption of deflationary measures, the process can be reversed. Immigration can stop and residents can start looking for better opportunities overseas; the inflow of capital might slow down; domestic capital might look across the borders for better and more secure returns; and the attempt through tougher deflationary measures, including monetary and capital controls, to restore the position, will only make things worse. The upward-spiralling gold-rush effect will be converted into a downward-spiralling worked-out-mine effect. Unless drastic measures are taken—roughly equivalent to, though not necessarily as inhuman as, the Berlin Wall—the worked-out-mine effect could become chronic.

One of the things that can cause the worked-out-mine effect is the extraction of capital and (perhaps temporarily) personnel from the economy in order to provide unrequited economic and technical aid, investment capital, defence aid, including supporting defence forces to the developing countries and, generally, in order to play a world political, economic and strategic role. It is not the only possible cause but it is a real and obvious one.

The risks are so great, that it is no wonder that fewer and fewer countries are prepared to run them. Soon there will be none. Certainly there will be none prepared to make outlays on the scale which the developing countries claim is necessary, unless arrangements are made which effectively eliminate the dangers of the worked-out-mine effect. It might be useful to look briefly, in the light of the gold-rush effect, at the impact on developing and 'recipient' countries of changes in migration and in the outflow of personnel and other resources from the developed countries.

The British experience contained, as noted above, a large emigration as well as, for a shorter period, a large concurrent immigration. Much of this emigration was to Australia which is another country which has sustained high employment and a high growth rate since the Second World War largely as a result of a high immigration rate. The Australian population in 1947 was about 7½ million. Twenty years later it was more than 11½ million—an increase of more than 53 per cent. Now it is more than 12½ million. Much of this was due to natural increase but at least half of it was due to immigration—more than 3 million people in twenty-five years, although this gross figure has been reduced by subsequent departures. This intake caused no problems of labour surplus. On the contrary, all the evidence is that it expanded consumer demand and investment to such an extent that it accentuated labour shortage. Successive Australian governments were faced with the problem, not of maintaining high levels of employment and economic activity but of keeping the boom within reasonable bounds.

The question for the future is whether immigration into Australia can be maintained. Availability of migrants from Western

Europe, which was high in the immediate post-war years and well into the fifties, was reduced greatly in the late fifties and sixties. Even the countries of southern Europe—especially Italy and Greece—are not now the seemingly inexhaustible source of migrants they once were. The earlier flood of migrants from Germany and Holland has now become little more than a trickle. Migration to Australia from France and Belgium has always been so small as to be almost negligible. In recent years, figures for immigration to Australia have been maintained only by an exceptional flow of migrants from Britain, reaching more than seventy thousand in some years. This British migration might continue, especially if prospects in Australia remain good, economic uncertainty persists in the United Kingdom and certain social difficulties associated with earlier coloured migration into Britain create social and psychological incentives to emigration, and, paradoxically, its continued restriction creates economic incentives to emigration.

However, if this migrant flow from Britain were seriously reduced, Australia could face serious difficulties. The economy has now been geared for a long time to a high migrant intake and, since the war, to a relatively high natural increase. The birthrate showed a marked decline for most of the sixties and the recent tendency to recover might be only temporary. Migration from Western Europe is unlikely to be renewed on a scale sufficient to compensate for a decline in the rate of population increase from other causes in the foreseeable future. If migration from Britain were to fall away therefore, Australia might be confronted with the prospect of a markedly reduced rate of population increase, and with the economic change of pace which that would entail. If the growth rate and the spontaneous high level of employment and economic activity were to decline, this in itself would be a further disincentive to immigration—and perhaps to an improvement in natural increase—and to investment whether from domestic sources or from overseas. A downward spiral might ensue which would call for more deliberate, stimulating efforts by the Government. In other words, after experiencing a gold-rush effect for a generation, Australia might be confronted with a situation similar to that which exists when the gold lodes are exhausted: no more people come to search for ore or mine it, people begin to move out and capital installations —houses, shops, hotels, local industries—begin to feel the pressure, and the less efficient, then the more efficient, no longer find a market and are left empty or go out of business. Just as the expansion in Australia was less dramatic and more solidly based than a gold rush, so any contraction is likely to be less sensational and less painful than the contraction when the gold lodes are exhausted. But the movement could be in the same direction and the process could be painful unless—and this seems likely in Australia's case—there are other elements, such as rapid and widespread mineral development, to maintain a robust dynamism.

How does the gold-rush effect have any relevance for the developing countries? If the thesis about the promptings to anti-colonialism is correct, the colonial powers once had an incentive to acquire, trade with and invest in the developing countries. But that was a transitory phase in the economic history of the now affluent economies. With the passing of this phase, there passed also any intense economic interest in the development of the underdeveloped countries; colonialism was brought to an end; and trade with and investment in the developing countries came to be of peripheral economic interest to the developed countries. The gold-rush effect of the colonial era started to bring many countries out of their traditional economic ways. Except in Japan, it never achieved the same results as in the countries where the industrial revolution originated. But the process having started, this process could have gathered great momentum as the developed countries moved at an ever higher rate to greater levels of production and productivity, if the developed countries had persisted with their economic interest in the developing countries. But the latter condition has not been met. The result has been that the gold-rush effect is now operating in reverse for the developing countries. Capital and labour are being concentrated in the developed world. In effect, there has been a decline in the 'natural' rate of flow of capital—and even a decline in the 'natural' rate of flow of personnel—to the developing countries. The latter have become an area where, for the developed countries, the 'gold lodes' have been worked out. Like many such areas in the affluent economies—especially former mining areas —efforts are made through what might be called international social services to maintain the developing world whose *raison d'etre* in economic terms has been so reduced. These international social services are the multilateral and bilateral aid, of a multitude of kinds, to which we have become increasingly accustomed and with which we have become increasingly preoccupied since the end of the Second World War.

IX
The Future Dynamism of the Developed

In the light of the accounts and the hypotheses which have so far been put forward, our next step is to consider the outlook for the highly developed countries, so many of which have undergone such a dynamic economic expansion in recent years. Among the more important issues to be considered are whether the most dynamic among them can maintain their economic dynamism and whether those countries which have experienced lesser growth and vitality can have their dynamism enhanced. With these questions is caught up the problem of maintaining stable growth and avoiding the recessions or the 'hesitations' in growth and employment of the past—recessions and 'hesitations' which have resulted, for the most part, from the belief of governments that certain deflationary policies have been necessary, at the upper level of the economy's activity, to restore internal and external equilibrium. And we must consider, in the light of the future dynamism and the future policies of the developed countries, how their economic relationships with the developing world are likely to evolve.

First of all, the tendency for population to concentrate in limited localities will probably persist. There will be intra-national concentrations, such as the movement of the British population from Scotland, Wales and the north of England into south-east England, the movement of German population to the Ruhr and other industrial areas, of French population to the industrial, commercial and service aggregations like Paris, and of Italian population to the north. There will also tend to be regional concentrations of population across national boundaries, the most notable being that contained in and around a 'golden[1] triangle' whose approximate points are London, Frankfurt and Paris and which covers the whole or part of six countries—Britain, France, Germany, Belgium, the Netherlands and Luxembourg. This concentration could be intensified if and when Britain becomes a member of the European Economic Community.

As we have already noted, one factor tending to encourage this concentration of population is the already considerable and still increasing part which service industries play in modern, high-living-standard economies. In most of these economies, tertiary industries employ more than half of the working population; and, by their very nature, most of them must be situated within the community they serve. If population moves to a certain area, service industries must expand to meet the increased demand, thus stimulating a further movement of population. The dynamics of the process are self-generating.

It is conceivable that an economic area could consist almost wholly of service industries. A capital city (such as Canberra) from which virtually all secondary industry is excluded could be an example of such an area. So also may be a region depending almost wholly on the tourist industry. These are extreme cases. But, with any high-living-standard economy, service industries will be important and, as living standards rise still further and as the economy grows, more consumer expenditure proportionately will be directed to services and proportionately less to the products of primary and secondary industry. This means that economic growth in a certain area will be less dependent on the existence of arable land and other natural resources in or near that area, and will be more dependent on density of population and the tendency for population density to increase. Deserts and dust bowls can, in theory, blaze everywhere like Las Vegas. There are some limits: Teheran, where almost two-thirds of Iran's gross national product other than oil is concentrated, and whose

[1] 'Golden' only in the sense of the wealth and economic power which it generates and not necessarily in the human environment which it provides.

population increased by 81 per cent in the 1960's, is said to be likely to suffer a shortage of water in the next twenty years as its population grows to five-and-a-half million. Therefore, establishment of further industries in and near Teheran is being limited by the government. But, while there are these other limits, the basic need for economic growth is people, whether as providers and consumers of services or, more generally, as producers and markets for their own (and others') production.

The movement of population from less dense to more dense areas will continue to cross national borders and could cause social problems, especially if it results in the congregation of large alien groups in limited areas. The problems will not be economic; and the social problems, in so far as they arise from the mingling of one European people with another, are likely to be much less intense than the problems created, for example, by the introduction of large communities of non-European migrants into Europe.

However, a high rate of movement of European peoples into areas of denser concentration cannot go on indefinitely. The reservoirs of labour are not unlimited.

There will of course continue to be some movement from the country to the urban areas. London's population has always taken large numbers of new citizens from the countryside. In the eighteenth and early nineteenth centuries, when surpluses of English wheat were recklessly converted into gin, the thousands of London's people slaughtered each year by the poisonous liquor sold at a multitude of low-class gin-shops, could be replaced only by large-scale migration from the countryside. The need to maintain the city's population against the ravages of poor-quality gin has passed, but cities—whose people tend to have a lower birth rate—still maintain and increase their numbers from the surplus which natural increase gives to the countryside. However, the numbers of people moving to urban areas in this way in the future are likely to be relatively small. And, apart from this small continuing source, the remaining reservoirs of labour in Western Europe are limited and are likely to run down further as each year passes.

Already the reservoirs have either been cut off, as from East Germany; or limitations on their tapping have been imposed or are in prospect, as, for example, in Greece; or the flow of labour has been too great in recent years to be sustained indefinitely even if no governmental restrictions are imposed. For example, the movement of southern Italian labour to northern Italy, Germany, France and the Benelux countries must eventually decline if only because the reservoirs, though large, cannot sustain it indefinitely.

The movement of southern Italian labour might also be increasingly concentrated on movement within Italy itself, provided northern, industrial Italy is able to maintain its lively growth. Reports towards the end of 1970 suggested that a new surge of south-to-north migration was in progress. This was described as a third wave, following the earlier large-scale migrations in 1955 and 1962—although migration on a less dramatic scale continued during the intervening years as well. Political, social and/or economic unrest in the south has caused these successive waves of migration, plus of course the attraction of the boom conditions in the north. During the 1970 third wave, the electronics, mechanical and rubber establishments in the Milan area recruited tens of thousands of workers—cheap, unskilled manpower—from the south. Arrivals of workers and their families in Milan from the south in the middle of the year were at the rate of about 200 to 300 a day; 50,000 arrived in Milan in the last quarter of 1970. More than six million southerners had moved from the south to the north between 1945 and 1970. Some satellite towns around such major industrial cities as Milan and Turin consist almost wholly of migrants from the south. But the migration of southern Italians, dramatic and large and persistent though it has been, must eventually come to an end. There might be a couple more waves yet but sooner or later the reservoir must be emptied and the migration must settle down to the normal country-urban migration characteristic of other modern European societies.

The reservoirs of labour in such countries as Spain and Turkey might have a longer life. But even these will fairly quickly dry up, if European growth rates and demand for labour are maintained at the levels of the 1960's, and if those countries now outside or less intensively inside the process of economic growth achieve the full dynamism of the currently most advanced Western European countries.

If concentration of labour within Europe slows or ceases, what will happen then? Broadly, one of four things could happen. First, a rising birth-rate in Western Europe could—theoretically or conceivably—provide the additional labour to offset declining immigration and so enable growth rates to continue at existing high levels. Second, productivity could increase to such an extent that, given adequate spread of income throughout the community, growth rates might be maintained at present high levels. Third, migrant labour might be obtained from outside Europe, perhaps initially from the Middle East, then from Asia, Africa and/or Latin America. Fourth, Governments might so be able to arrange matters that, despite a static working population, employment and growth rates can be maintained at high levels indefinitely.

Let us examine each of these possibilities in turn. First, a rising birth-rate in Europe seems—at the moment—an especially unlikely prospect. The advent of simple and reliable contraceptives, especially oral contraceptives, and a more relaxed attitude to abortion, have already reduced the birth-rate in the more sophisticated economies, in some cases to a level even lower than that prevailing in the worst depths of the thirties depression. Newer and more efficient contraceptives and easier abortion are likely to affect most importantly those lower-age groups from whom, because, *inter alia*, of a dramatic reduction in the average age of marriage, any increase in the birth-rate would be most likely to come. Thus, the present prospect is that a reduction in the flow of immigrant labour into the highly industrialised areas of Western Europe could be concurrent with a decline in the birth-rate to or perhaps even below replacement levels. If this were to happen and total population were to be virtually static, the rate of future economic growth would be much more heavily dependent on technological progress. This might be considerable but might be well below the growth rates of 4 per cent or 5 per cent per annum in real terms which have been regarded as unexceptional in recent years. Even a marked reduction in the *rate* of increase of the employed population could cause marked changes in the economy's growth rate, in the importance of technological advances and in public policy. For example, if the present rate of growth of Britain's population, which had fallen from about 500,000 a year in 1960 to about 250,000 in 1969 were to fall still further, this would seem to require the British Government to take even more active measures than it has already to try to improve the economy's growth rate, to stimulate technological progress and to give greater strength to the country's balance-of-payments position through adjustments, for example, to its East-of-Suez and other 'world-role' policies.[2]

The second possibility is that there might be a rise in productivity. This is more than a possibility; it is a virtual certainty. However, the technical capacity to improve productivity is not the same as the economic and social capacity fully to realise it. If aggregate demand is growing rapidly, if labour is short, if the incentives to invest are at a maximum, increases in productivity will move more rapidly towards their full technical potential. But if aggregate demand is static or increasing only slowly, if the labour supply is ample and if the incentives for new investment are consequently modest, the technical potential for increases in productivity will be much less completely realised. Not only will there be economic disincentives but social considerations will also lead in the direction of retarding technical changes which could enlarge productivity. In other words, a downward spiral arising from failure of the economy to grow through increases in the working and consuming population could be reinforced by a reduced rate of improvement in productivity. This does not mean that there will not be some improvement in productivity; a slackening demand for labour and the creation of a larger pool of unemployed is likely to increase productivity per worker with existing equipment, although aggregate production might decline. But a downward spiral could lead to an

[2] Some people adopt an exactly contrary line of argument. A British Government report issued in January 1970 predicted that Britain's population might reach 68 million by the end of the century. Even though this was well below the prediction of 74.7 million made by the Oversea Migration Board in 1964, the 1970 report said that every aspect of Britain's life would be under pressure through the dramatic population increase. Sir Solly Zuckerman, who headed the enquiry which produced the report, was reported to have said that the increase would make it more difficult to find jobs, homes, hospital beds, and school places and that the Government would be under strong pressure for birth-control measures. The absurdity of this economic reasoning can be partially excused only because it may have had some validity thirty or fifty years ago and it is still the conventional wisdom of a great number of otherwise intelligent people.

overall result of a decline both in production and in the rate of improvement of productivity; and the growth rate would consequently be depressed well below the level which would be realised if significant numbers of new workers were being drawn into an already fully employed economy. It would need an improvement of techniques at a rate markedly in advance of that of recent years to maintain present growth rates with a static working population. In addition, it would call for government policies of much greater scope and determination than recently to maintain full employment and get a high realisation of technological potential, if the employed population remains static or nearly so.

The third possibility—migration from sources outside Europe—theoretically offers greater—indeed, virtually unlimited—results in terms of economic growth. If the 'gold-rush' theory is valid, migration to industrial centres brings benefits both to the immigrants and those already there. It increases commodity demand, adds value to—or realises the full potential of—existing investment and stimulates further investment, provides additional demand for (and supply of) services which constitute the major part of modern economic output, and supplies the labour by means of which a high rate of economic growth can most easily be achieved, maintained or increased. As the nearer sources of labour become exhausted, it would be logical, in economic terms, for the highly industrialised countries to look to, let us say, Asia or the Middle East, or the traditional migrant flow to Latin America might be reversed, so as to bring Latin American labour to Europe. Ultimately, logic and economic benefit might suggest that labour be drawn from wherever it is available, if necessary from the most distant and isolated parts of Asia and Africa.

There is little doubt that, in economic terms, the highly developed economies of the North Atlantic Community could readily absorb this labour in considerable volume and for many years to come; and that these highly developed economies would benefit from it. In fact, as we have already noted, the flow of labour would in itself help to create the conditions needed to sustain it. Equally, there is no doubt—still thinking solely in economic terms—that the immigrants would obtain considerable economic benefits from their migration. Their labour, which is their only resource and which is of little value in the labour-surplus economies of their origin, would be of higher value in the labour-scarce economies of their migration; and its value would tend to be related to the value attributed to the equivalent domestic labour in the countries of immigration—a value established during a long period of advancing economic and social welfare and during the long history of trade-union industrial struggle in the highly developed economies. The natural economic forces behind this flow of migrant labour would seem to be so great that, if other restraints were removed, the problem would be to control it and to make arrangements for sufficient investment in housing and other facilities in the industrial countries comfortably to contain it. If the non-economic restraints were removed, this problem of expanding social investment would preoccupy the governments of receiving countries. Once the movement had begun, they would need to concern themselves hardly at all with maintaining immigration at a level sufficient to sustain a high rate of growth in their economies.

However, this ready-made resolution of a supply-and-demand problem cannot be regarded solely in economic terms. If the world population were homogeneous or no less homogeneous than the populations of, let us say, Spain and Germany, the problem might be a manageable one; although even these differences introduce social difficulties into migration if it continues at a high level over many years. The chances of maintaining a high rate of migration for a long time between countries with markedly heterogenous populations and distinct racial differences, and at the same time maintaining social harmony, would seem to be small.

There are two main reasons for this. The first has nothing necessarily to do with race; it derives from the intolerable concentration of population which continuing migration could cause. The concentration of population in the 'Golden Triangle' of south-east England, Belgium, Holland, south-west Germany and north-west France is already intense. No doubt, this concentration will become still greater; and a considerable inflow of population and investment could take place before the area becomes, as one imagines it might, one vast metropolis: a metropolis in which the cities of London, Paris, Brussels, Antwerp, Rotterdam, Amsterdam, Dusseldorf, Essen, Cologne and the rest would continue to encroach on and engulf the villages, towns and cities in their vicinities. But is there not a limit to this concentration? If it goes on indefinitely will the area—and other areas like Tokyo—not strangle themselves into stagnation? Much will depend on the extent to which new ways can be found to make high-density concentrations of population tolerable, and to lower the costs of congestion in relation to the savings from concentration of supplies, markets and services.

The second reason is more closely connected with racial differences. Some large communities can easily absorb fairly large numbers of other nationalities and race. The large student communities in Western European countries, for example, have been able to accommodate African and Asian groups without strain. Here however there is a certain homogeneity of intellect and activity which, quite apart from the relatively small numbers involved, makes absorption comparatively easy. But much depends on the numbers involved, the permanence or otherwise of residence and the extent to which they can be socially integrated with the rest of the community. If the numbers are so large and residence is so permanent that separate, alien communities tend to be formed in the original community to contain them, a problem of a quite different order arises from the absorption of students of different races in a single university campus.

Immigration of large numbers of Asians and Africans solely for the purpose of selling their labour is likely to cause problems of this quite different order. Their common ground—socially and in terms of living standards—with the indigenous population might be small; and their concentration in the lower levels of the income range is likely to attract attention both to their numbers and to their social differences. A likely ghetto style of living would tend to perpetuate and accentuate these differences. As we have said, the problems would not be economic; but the homogeneity of European populations could be so disturbed that racial antipathies and conflicts would quickly develop. In the host countries, their presence would arouse resentments against the alleged deterioration of indigenous social standards. In the countries of origin, the movement of large numbers of their

people into situations of social and racial inferiority might ultimately create deep feelings of discrimination and even give some
sense of a revival, in modern form, of a 'slave trade' by the white
and rich countries involving the poor and coloured peoples. A
great deal of emotion and a great deal of irrational thinking
would be likely to be involved on both sides.

The British experience of recent years may be indicative. There
was no pressure by the countries of emigration to stop the flow
of coloured migrants to Britain. On the contrary, these countries
objected only to the restrictions which were imposed by the
British Government on continuing, unlimited migration. These
restrictions were regarded as a form of discrimination. Nevertheless, objections to this form of discrimination must be balanced
against the objections which would be voiced—and have been
voiced—about discrimination and ill-treatment when large
numbers of coloured migrants continue to live in Britain at the
bottom of the social and economic ladder and continue to form
a separate and distinctive depressed minority in the larger white
community. Objections about ill-treatment would intensify still
further as animosities between the original and the alien communities deepened.

In the light of the British experience, it seems unlikely that
Western European countries will seek to satisfy their needs for
extra labour by substantial migration from outside the European
frontiers. If this migration were to start on any scale, the British
experience would be likely to be repeated, that is, after a period
of heavy immigration, restrictions would be imposed as social
problems intensified.

The fourth possibility—that Governments might be able so to
arrange matters that, despite a static working population, employment and growth rates can be maintained indefinitely at
high levels—is not without reality. If the working population is
increasing, high levels of employment and high growth rates will
be easier to maintain. But their maintenance may still be practicable even with a static population. Ordinarily, high growth
rates with a static working population would be dependent on
improvements in technology leading to improvements in productivity. Even without improvements in technology or other
changes, high levels of employment could be held under a

Keynesian system although more positive and more sustained efforts by Governments would be necessary, in most countries, than in recent years. In other words, the deliberate effort might be more constantly to maintain internal and external equilibrium without precipitating a recession than, as so frequently in so many countries in recent years, to keep a steadying hand on a highly dynamic growth situation.

There are other possibilities. Aggregate labour resources should not be computed simply by tallying population of working age. Rather are they a function of both numbers and skills; and unemployment may exist, even though it may not be recorded, if actual or potential skills are not used where they are most efficient. Equally, there is actual unemployment or underemployment if numbers or skills are used at less than their full capacity. This sort of unemployment or underemployment undoubtedly exists in all highly developed countries and in recent years, has shown some tendency to increase. It exists both in agriculture and industry.

Therefore, one of the ways in which economic growth may be achieved even in a static-population, fixed-technology situation[3], is to move labour and capital from less efficient to more efficient uses. It is not only the developing countries which allocate factors of production to inefficient uses. If only because a high level of employment and income allows an economy to carry more burdens—of certain kinds and within certain limits—the developed countries not only allow uneconomic production to continue but actively encourage and support it. Transfers of labour from this uneconomic production could lift productivity and growth rates, and they could affect the relationships between the developed and the developing countries. We shall examine these possible transfers in more detail a little later.

They are one means of using more profitably the labour which is already available. There is another means of increasing production and income with the labour which is already available in the economy. That is to use it more intensively. This more inten-

---

[3] This is not to say that we are inevitably confronted with a static population and fixed technology in the developed economies over any long period of time. The population seems likely to grow slowly in most, if not all, developed countries but improvement in technology is equally likely to be rapid.

sive use of available labour could not only expand production and income but it could also be one of the fundamental short-term, as well as long-term, stabilisers of the economy and, in certain circumstances, could solve, at least in part, the problem of making more resources available to the developing countries. Let us have a look at these possibilities in a little more detail.

As productivity has advanced in the developed countries and as trade-union power has grown, working hours have been reduced and so has the proportion of the population employed for wages in the economy. Married women do not work. Nor do the young or the old. The young stay at school and university much longer than they did not merely 100 years ago but even ten or twenty years ago. A higher and higher proportion of the young now seek paid employment only when they graduate from university in the early or mid-twenties. For the old, there is a tendency for them to retire earlier—at sixty or less, rather than sixty-five—and they live much longer after retirement than they did a generation and more ago. For the employed, the award working-week has been reduced in most countries to forty hours and the actual hours worked, including overtime, have moved down towards forty in most countries. An accompanying table shows how working hours have declined in selected countries in recent years. The trade unions are engaged in a campaign in many countries to reduce the award working-week to thirty-five hours. Apart from reduction of the working-week, annual leave, furlough and sick-leave arrangements are now much more generous than they were. So are unemployment benefits.

There are some qualifications to be made to the above. Some married women do work. Some students work during part of their time at school or university, for example, during vacations. Some people, especially the self-employed, do not retire at sixty or sixty-five but work until they are seventy or eighty or even more.

But the general rule is that a small and declining proportion of the population is providing more and more income from a shorter and shorter working schedule. The exceptions to this general rule provide the clue to the way in which the general rule might be modified to achieve greater production, greater stability and greater happiness—in so far as that can be identified and measured—for everyone.

Production can be varied considerably by comparatively small percentage changes in the employed population or, more accurately, in the aggregate labour unit time worked. Out of a total population of ten million in a typical advanced economy, about four million are actually working for wages, salary and other forms of monetary compensation—and each employee is working for about forty hours each week.

If immigration into our typical economy were achieved at the very high rate of 2 per cent of the population, it would add 200,000 people to the population each year. Not all of these immigrants would in fact add to the employed labour force; many of them would be wives and children and other unemployed or unemployable members of the family. But, for present purposes, let us assume that they would all be employed and that each would add to production on average the same as the average worker already in the economy. Then the 200,000 migrants (constituting 5 per cent of the employed labour force) would add 5 per cent to the gross national product. If the GNP were $20 billion, they would add $1 billion to the gross national product. If the migrant intake had been 400,000 (4 per cent of the existing population or 10 per cent of the employed population), the increase in the gross national product would have been $2 billion; if it had been 500,000 (5 per cent of the total population or 12½ per cent of the working population), it would have been $2½ billion.

Much the same sort of result—there are some important qualifications—can be achieved by a changed utilisation of labour resources already existing in the economy. If the present working week were taken to be forty hours, production and therefore gross national product and gross national income could be increased by 2 per cent or $400 million if the working week went up to forty hours forty-eight minutes, by 4 per cent or $800 million if the working week went up to forty-one hours thirty-six minutes, and by 5 per cent of $1 billion if the working week went up to forty-two hours.

There is evidence to suggest that, although the working week has been formally reduced over the last couple of decades, the actual hours of work for each worker have remained much the same or have been reduced only very little—indeed, in some cases they have increased—in the last fifteen years or so. The hours worked above the formal working week are presumably paid for mainly at overtime rates, so that what workers have been seeking in a reduction of the working week is not so much an increase in leisure as an increase in remuneration.

The attached table shows that, in Australia, where unions have traditionally been strong and labour conditions have been of the highest standards and where a forty-hour working week was introduced shortly after the Second World War, the average hours worked in 1963 were 42.8 and, by 1968, they had *risen* to 43.7. In the United States, much the same trend occurred. In 1953, the actual hours of work per worker were 40.5. This figure fell to a low of 39.7 in 1960, rose to a high of 41.4 in 1966 and was 40.7—still above the 1953 figure—in 1968. Both Australia and the United States experienced dynamic economic growth during the sixties. Britain, on the other hand, had a difficult decade; and average hours actually worked by each worker fell there from 47.4 in 1960 for males to a low of 45 in 1966 and up to 45.8 in 1968. For women, hours fell from 40.4 in 1960 to a low of 38 in 1966 and 1967 and moved up slightly to 38.2 in 1968. Although in Britain hours worked therefore declined, the decline was small and hours worked, especially for males, remained high—higher indeed than in Australia or the United States.

Generally, the following table shows that hours actually worked have remained fairly constant and there is some evidence that maintenance of or a tendency to upward movement in the hours worked is associated with dynamic economic conditions and robust good health in the economy. Certainly, there is little evidence to suggest that economic dynamism and general robustness of the economy are linked with a reduction—far less a marked reduction—in the hours actually worked.

Shorter working hours, or more leisure, might be less important than a greater freedom for the individual worker to make use of his time. A recent experiment by a manufacturer in the United States showed a rise in efficiency when the working day was increased to nine hours but the working week was reduced to four days. This brought incidental advantages to the company in getting their product to market, and the workers were delighted with the three-day weekend. Professor Paul Samuelson, in

HOURS ACTUALLY WORKED PER WEEK PER WORKER IN MANUFACTURING

Country	1953	1960	Low Point	1968
Austria	44.0	43.5	42.5 (1963)	43.7
Australia		42.8 (1963)	42.8 (1963)	43.7
Canada	41.3	40.4	40.3 (1967)	40.3
France	—	45.7	45.4 (1967)	45.3
Germany	48.0	45.6	42.0 (1967)	43.0
Ireland	45.1	45.4	43.6 (1967)	43.7
Japan	—	47.8	44.3 (1965)	44.6
New Zealand	—	40.4	40.2 (1961-2-7)	40.2
Switzerland	47.7	46.1	44.6 (1968)	44.6
United Kingdom	—	Males 47.4	45.0 (1966)	45.8
	—	Females 40.4	38.0 (1966-7)	38.2
United States	40.5	39.7	39.7 (1960)	40.7

Source: *United Nations Statistical Yearbook, 1969*

applauding the shorter working week, is alleged to have repeated his belief that leisure should be included in the calculation of the gross national product. While that may be conceded, it is doubtful how far the workers would use their four-day week or would have welcomed their four-day week solely because of the promise it gave for leisure. What it did do, however, was to release the men for almost half the week for other activities, some of which might have been as remunerative as their original factory work. Their week was now better organised, giving them more freedom and making them both more efficient in their four-day week and poten-tially more productive—in market as well as leisure hours— outside it. It is with this variety of considerations in mind that an adjustment of the working week should be regarded.

By and large, it is this more intensive use of existing labour *already employed* within the economy which can probably be most effective in raising production and thereby in stabilising the economy at the upper level of activity. An increase in pro-ductivity and production, for example, through increased working time, of the *regular work force* is likely to add most to aggregate production and, therefore, to gross national product. But there are alternative sources of labour which can also be used to increase production—probably as a supplement to, rather than as a substitute for, already employed labour. These alternative sources would mean that new labour would be drawn into the economy.

For example, although many married women now work, most do not. In our theoretical economy of ten million total population and four million working population, we shall assume that initially no married women work and that there are two million married women in the total population. If now one in ten of these married women, that is, a total of 200,000 were to accept full-time paid employment, that would increase the labour force of four million by 5 per cent and the gross national product would increase by $1 billion from $20 billion to $21 billion. If one in five of the married women worked half-time, the increase in the gross national product would be the same $1 billion or if they worked full time, it would increase by 10 per cent or $2 billion.

The same sort of general result can be achieved by absorbing into the economy some of those who are now considered either too old or too young to work. In our theoretical national economy of ten million, about 10 per cent or one million (including both men and women) are over sixty. If one in five of these older people can be brought into paid employment, they will increase the labour force and the gross national product by the same amount as 200,000 immigrants or 200,000 married women newly entering paid employment.

Moreover, older people have advantages in terms of efficiency over either immigrants or (sometimes) younger married women. They are often highly skilled, have a long employment experience and are more reliable, less choosey and willing to work for less than younger workers. The United States Bureau of Labor Statistics estimates that, of the 20 million Americans over the age of sixty-five, about 2 million or one in ten hold jobs. Most of these are self-employed or employed in volunteer work or small family-type businesses without retirement rules or pension benefits. Some of the twenty million would be too frail or ill to accept regular employment—although some employees are now being newly hired in the United States aged eighty to eighty-five and even up to ninety. Certainly three or four times as many old people could be employed as are employed now. That is, instead of 2 million Americans over sixty-five holding jobs, the number could be as high as 6 or 8 or perhaps even 10 million.

In Australia, out of more than one million people over sixty-five probably about half a million would be ready and willing to work if the opportunities and incentives were there and the disincentives were not. Since, at present, only about 120,000 people over sixty-five are included in the labour force, employment of older people able and willing to work would probably increase the total labour force by something like 8 per cent. The willingness of the older worker seems to be beyond doubt: he is often so eager to work that he will not complain about conditions which would cause a younger worker to run. 'The older worker may go at a slower pace,' said an American employer, 'but over a year's time, you get more out of him because he's more steady, conscientious and always shows up for work.' This was confirmed by another employer who said, 'We found that the seniors did as good a job, and in some instances better, than our young contemporaries.'

The opportunities for the older worker are still not great— although they are growing—because there is still a prejudice against him and an unfounded belief that he cannot stand up to regular employment. When he is employed, incentives tend to be low because he tends to be poorly paid and to be placed in the least interesting, most routine positions. But probably the greatest barrier to employment of the older worker is not a lack of incentives but the existence of powerful disincentives, particularly arising from the older worker's probable loss of pension payments if he takes a job or, in any event, if he earns more than a certain amount. In the United States, the older worker's Social Security payments are halved if he earns more than $1680 a year and they disappear entirely if he earns more than $2880. In Australia, the old person's pension starts to be reduced if he earns more than about $500 and is lost completely by the time he earns $1500.

If disincentives could be removed and—although this seems less necessary—if additional incentives could be provided, employment of older people could probably expand employment by about—or up to—10 per cent and could add something like 10 per cent—perhaps more—to the gross national product.

The possibilities of moving more of the younger people into paid employment are probably a great deal less than those for married women and older people. The modern economy needs a

high proportion of its labour force to have a high level of professional and technical qualifications. A long period of training for
large numbers of people before they enter paid employment is
therefore unavoidable. Any attempt to interfere fundamentally
with this arrangement would only bring economic deterioration.

However, some greater contribution to immediate production
by the student sector of the population might be possible and
could probably be achieved if incentives were provided and
organisation were better. Long university vacations especially
might be organised in such a way as to add to aggregate production in the economy.

The important thing is that our economic policy does not pay
sufficient attention to production. It is concerned primarily with
employment (and unemployment) and demand, with per capita
income and with that grand and glorious aggregate in modern
economics, gross national product. Galbraith, one of the more
popular but also one of the more imaginative of modern economists, tends to contest this. 'The Great Depression,' he wrote,
'brought production to a very low level. Between 1929 and 1933
the gross product of the private economy dropped by between a
third and a half. The sheer magnitude of this movement focused
attention, as never before, on movements in the total output of
the economy and on their far-reaching consequences for economic
and political fortune. Characteristically, to increase production was
less central to men's thoughts than to reduce unemployment. "Our
greatest primary task is to put people back to work," Roosevelt
said in his first inaugural. But whether directly or as a by-product
of the effort to reduce economic insecurity, expanded production
began to acquire a growing significance to political liberalism
in its American sense. Then in 1936 came John Maynard Keynes.
In the Keynesian system the notion of an aggregate demand for
the output of the economy which determined the total production
of the economy was central . . . by manipulating the level of
aggregate demand . . . the government could influence the level
of production.'[4]

We would say rather that unemployment and demand have
remained as the variables which have preoccupied 'liberal'
governments during the Keynesian period. Even gross national

[4] Galbraith, *The Affluent Society*, pp. 147-8

product comes out as an incident derived from the other variables of employment and demand with which economic policy is concerned, rather than as a deliberate target at which policy aims. There is little sense of deciding that, for example, a gross national product of $50 billion is needed to realise all the internal and external needs of an economy and to do so while maintaining stable prices. Perhaps the developed market economies think that this comes too close to socialistic national planning; but, in fact, it calls for no more planning than is already undertaken in the often unsuccessful attempt to maintain or restore full employment or stable prices. Little attention is given to the conception of the way in which production—not productivity but just simple production—can be increased by drawing new labour into employment or reduced by allowing labour to leave employment. Employment and unemployment are varied from time to time, not with an eye on production, but in order to vary demand by reducing or expanding personal incomes.

So there is little understanding of the labour resources in the economy which are not used, or not used regularly, but which could be used, if need be, to meet the economy's requirements for increased production. Just as one—and certainly not the most important—illustration of the wide range of unused labour resources, every economy has a large number of disabled persons who are eager and would be able to work if arrangements were made for them. Last year in the United States 200,000 disabled persons were found and rehabilitated; but, while this was happening, a further 300,000 persons became disabled. So, despite the great effort, the gap between those disabled and those rehabilitated grew by 100,000. Some of these people would be beyond substantial rehabilitation; but very few would be beyond any rehabilitation. Here then is another group in the economy which could be drawn back to some extent into production and which would enjoy social and psychological benefit from it. It could not be a major factor in increasing the gross national product or stabilising the economy nor could it be subject to the same periodic incentives and disincentives which should be applied, for reasons of stability, to other groups in the economy. But it does illustrate the extent of the unutilised labour in the economy which could be used, not in a way which would damage the society or the individual, but in a way which would be of great benefit to both.

If currently unused labour resources were more fully utilised in this way, the labour force might be increased by about one-third and the gross national product increased by the same amount. A gross national product of $20 billion could be increased by $6 billion to, let us say, $26 billion by these means. There are however some qualifications to be made to these broad-brush estimates of gain. First, the additions to the labour force will not necessarily be able to make the same addition to production per unit of labour as the labour force already at work within the economy. Additional hours worked by the existing labour force could have much the same value although, if anything, it will be less; and married women and older employees will tend to be less skilled or less dynamic or, in any event, to do work at the lower end of the wages scale.

Secondly, however, additions made to production will not be a simple measure of the additional labour units multiplied by their wages. The additional product will be their labour enhanced by the capital with which they work. Much of the capital of the economy is under-utilised because of the shortness of the working week. If the additional labour resources extend the hours of work or allow the more complete utilisation of land, buildings and equipment within existing hours of work, this could mean that product can be increased without any additional creation of capital being necessary to enable the most efficient employment of the new labour.

Third, the trend towards paid employment of more married women and older persons seems already to be well established. There also seems to be some evidence that those regularly in employment seek additional work, so that they have either two jobs or one full-time job and a part-time job. 'Moonlighting' is becoming less an eccentricity in some communities than a habit and a way of life. Not only is there the possibility of increasing the gross national product through the more complete utilisation of existing labour resources; but economic and social attitudes may already have been established within the community consistent with arrangements to draw unused labour into the enonomy. This is vital. To take an existing trend in order to direct and adapt it will be much easier than to attempt to create a trend anew or reverse an existing one.

We will need more evidence to establish, with absolute assurance for all groups, this willingness to work more (and, of course, to earn more). But at least there is some evidence which can be immediately adduced, for example, to show that some workers are seeking earlier retirement benefits, not in order to stop working, but in order to increase income by adding a pension to current, earned wages. In November 1970, General Motors reached an agreement with the United Auto Workers Union which provided, *inter alia*, for retirement on pension at a certain age after a minimum of thirty years' service. 'The economics of the proposed arrangement in the new contract are dubious enough,' said *The Wall Street Journal* on 18 November 1970. 'Beginning October 1 1971, workers who are fifty-eight years old with thirty years of service can retire with a $500-a-month pension. Beginning October 1 1972, the age requirement will drop to fifty-six from fifty-eight. Under the old contract the best pension was $400 a month at age sixty. Direct costs of such pensions plainly will be considerable, although the exact outlays will depend on the number of employees who retire early. The number of such plans, in public as well as private employment, is growing, and the experience to date suggests that a sizable portion of the workers who gain eligibility do make use of it. In theory, retirement and pension programs are attempts to offset the economic costs of old age. The pensioner left the labour force and, with Social Security and his retirement cheque, lived out his days. But is that what has happened, and will happen, with the trend toward ever earlier retirement? . . . The worker at fifty-five or sixty can on the average look forward to more added years of healthy, productive life than was the case two or three decades ago. Will this worker voluntarily quit the labor force? . . . The economy can and should make adequate arrangements to care for the elderly. The ill-advised push for ever-earlier retirement, however, is making it more difficult to provide such arrangements. It is surely ironic that this push is coming at the same time as fresh efforts to bar job discrimination on the basis of age.'

The main concern of *The Wall Street Journal* was the burden which higher and earlier pension payments placed on the economy; but of much more real significance was the Journal's recognition that fewer and fewer pensionable employees were likely in fact to discontinue working after they had taken their pensions. If workers did in fact cease to be producers at the age of fifty-six or fifty-eight, the burden on the economy would be enormous. But if earlier 'retirement' helps to establish social habits of continuing to work after receipt of pension, the effect might be not to reduce but to increase the community's production and thus not to increase but to reduce the burdens which the older age-groups place on the other, traditionally more productive age-groups in the community.

However, much more important even than the contribution to the gross national product is the vital role which the more complete utilisation of labour can play in stabilising the economy. It is this role which could mean that the Keynesian system which has brought so many benefits could now be brought to realise its full potential. It could mean that the instability which has so far been experienced at the upper employment level of the economy and which has led to a reduction in dynamism and production could be eliminated. How can this be managed?

To answer this, we must go back to the fundamentals of the Keynesian system. That system was designed to meet the situation of the depressed 1930's. It was intended, in a situation of cyclical and, in some measure, chronic depression resulting from a failure of demand, to stimulate that demand and so move the economy back to levels of full employment. As demand and employment increased so did production until it hit against the ceiling of full employment. In theory, at that point, demand would have levelled off—or desirably we would have hoped that it would have levelled off—so that demand and supply would be nicely in equilibrium at full employment of the economy.

Unfortunately, that sort of perfect equilibrium was rarely achieved. Even when it was achieved, it was rarely maintained. Up to a point, this was both understandable and acceptable. The fiscal and monetary stimuli used to move the economy upwards could not be expected to hit their target with absolute precision, especially given not only the technical factors but also the human factors, including those of confidence or lack of it, which enter into the situation. The odds were that, if government policies were to hit their target, they would probably carry some way beyond it.

The key words were 'some way'. Most governments have been prepared to accept some degree of excess of demand over supply, leading to a degree of inflation. As experience has grown, a 'creeping' inflation of 1 per cent or 2 per cent or even 3 per cent each year has come to be regarded as an inevitable and acceptable accompaniment of Keynesian policies. But only so much inflation could be permitted, especially when this inflation was a symptom of some serious disequilibrium which often expressed itself in other ways as well, for example, in imbalance in the external payments.

So, from time to time, governments felt themselves compelled to take action to stop inflation and restore balance to the economy. Sometimes they decided that a 'fundamental disequilibrium' existed in the economy and altered the exchange rate. Mostly, however, they assumed that, since the fiscal and monetary stimuli which they had used to expand demand had created excessive demand, the obvious solution was to reverse the stimuli. Since, however, there has been an increasing reluctance to return to anything like the depressed conditions which originally called the stimuli forth, the reversal of policies was allowed to cause some unemployment and some reduction in demand, but demand showed a growing susceptibility to fall less than production. So that reversal of fiscal and monetary stimuli then meant both more unemployment and more inflation—and not much, if any, help to the balance of payments, indeed, sometimes the contrary.

The accompanying chart on p. 126 shows dramatically what happened to the United States economy in the first nine months of 1970. Deflationary policies were in operation by the Nixon Administration in an effort to stop inflation in the domestic economy and to improve the country's external economic position. As a result, unemployment rose from less than 4 per cent in January 1970 to more than 5½ per cent only nine months later in October 1970, when there were 4.3 million people unemployed. But, despite this terrifying rise in unemployment, the cost of living rose by 4.8 points—round about 4 per cent— from an index below 132 in January 1970, to a figure not much short of 137 in September 1970. During this period, the United States got just about the worst of the possible economic worlds available to it. It got less employment than it should have done—and than it had become used to; it got less production than it should have done; and it paid nevertheless a lot more money than it should have for what it got. On the surface at least, the deflationary policies of the Nixon Administration, as they had worked out towards the end of 1970, looked as though they left a lot to be desired.

UNEMPLOYMENT RATE UP

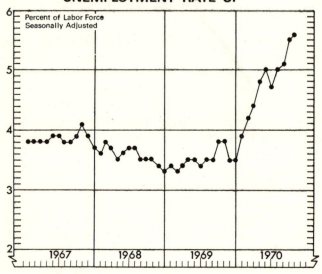

Source: The Wall Street Journal, 9 November 1970

The position has been the same in Britain. Deflation has not achieved equilibrium either internally or externally and, during 1970, wage inflation created an awesome threat to the economy, despite the fact that unemployment was relatively high by recent British standards and the growth in the economy remained low (perhaps an increase of 1½ per cent annually in the real gross national product). Indeed, these two things—which meant that labour's rewards were less (and less certain)—plus a rise of 7 per cent in retail prices during the previous year, while productivity rose by only 3 per cent, production by only 1 per

TWO PROBLEMS THAT ARE PLAGUING THE ECONOMY

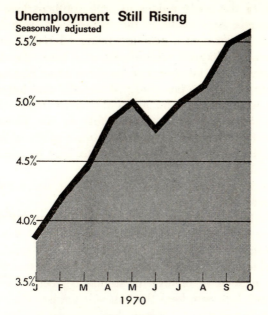

Unemployment Still Rising
Seasonally adjusted

1970

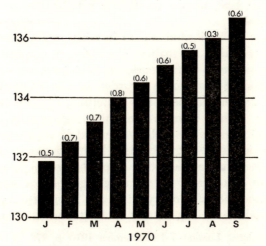

Cost of Living Still Rising
1957-59=100, all items

Figures in parentheses indicate increase over previous month.

1970

Source: The New York Times, 8 November 1970

cent and employment fell by 2-3 per cent, almost certainly acted as stimuli to the trade unions to seek compensation in higher wage demands. As a result, at the end of 1970, 'wage awards of more than 15 per cent a year are being offered in occupations with generally adequate recruitment, at a time when real gross national product so far this year has been rising at or around an annual rate of only 1½ per cent'.[5] While this threatened to have terrifying results in Britain, much the same trend—though yet on a less terrifying scale—was visible in the United States. Policies of throttling back demand—quite futilely in the light of other policies—were thus threatening to lead to real economic disaster.

What is wrong with these policies? What alternative policies should have been adopted?

What is in fact needed to restore equilibrium at the upper, inflationary level of the modern, Keynesian economy is not more unemployment but less unemployment, not less production but more production. The only target which the present British and American policies of reversal of stimuli correctly aimed at was less demand, but even here the aim was wrong. The aim should have been to achieve not simply less demand in absolute terms but less demand in relation to production and supply. To attempt to reduce demand without paying close attention to the simultaneous effect of policies on production and supply was to court failure or, at best, to rely on chance whether the policies succeeded or not.

What was really needed was to increase production. Under a Keynesian system, in the mature, free-enterprise economies, there is as we have already noted, curiously little emphasis on the level of production. It tends to be regarded as a result of an increase in demand and employment; it is something which occurs almost incidentally, rather than as something deliberately aimed at. Even though there is the highest approval of a high growth rate, this rate tends to be regarded as a happy outcome of demand policies rather than a realisation of production objectives.

Therefore, apart from the seeming logic of reversing policies which created the inflationary crisis, any habit of direct stimulation of production is generally lacking and this may be an

[5] *The Economist*, London, 7-13 November 1970, p. 17

inhibiting factor in dealing with a disequilibrium at the upper, inflationary level of the economy. But that does not alter the fact that the correct solution at that point is to increase production, while at the same time keeping demand in check. If practicable, demand should be reduced or held at existing levels, but, in any event, it should not be allowed to increase as fast as production.

How do you increase production when the economy is already in a condition of full employment? The obvious answer is that you can't, and to revert therefore to the policies of reducing demand which have failed in the past. But there is an alternative. Production *can* be increased.

The critical point is when the economy has moved up to full employment, demand has continued at a high level and production has hit a ceiling thus causing inflationary pressures. If the pressures continue, there will be a spiralling effect and inflation will get out of hand. At as early a stage as possible, therefore, after the inflationary pressures are identified or can be seen to be developing, policies should be implemented to increase production while holding back demand.

These policies might be along the following lines:

1 Taxation concessions should be given to companies and other employers—perhaps in special sectors of production; perhaps universally—which expand their employment and/or production beyond a base-year level;

2 Tax incentives should be given to those already employed to work longer hours and take additional jobs; employers should be given taxation and perhaps other fiscal incentives to offer overtime work and to take on second-job workers;

3 Older persons (those beyond retirement and pensionable age) should be encouraged to take paid employment; their pension rights should not be affected by this employment; for example, any means test for a government pension should be suspended during a designated period of employment; their earnings might be taxed at a concessional rate; and a wage supplement or tax concession might be granted to employers of older persons;

4 Married women should be encouraged to take paid employment; tax deductions allowable to married couples should be

continued during this employment; married women's earnings should be taxed at a concessional rate, perhaps up to a certain level and for a certain period, say twelve months, after which the concession may or may not be renewable; a wage supplement or tax concession might be paid to employers of married women (perhaps only if they must accept special conditions of work, such as work for limited hours or for only three or four days a week); special arrangements should be made by the government to enable married women to take paid employment, for example, additional child-minding centres might be established;

5 As an accompaniment especially to overtime and second-job employment, companies might be induced (by, for example, reduction of company taxes on additional revenue) to utilise their capital more fully by, for example, instituting longer hours of factory or store operation or shift work for continuous production;

6 Special training arrangements might be established by the government for married women re-entering or entering employment for the first time, for older persons needing new skills or refreshment of old ones and for already employed workers who need a second skill for a second job;

7 Any increases in government expenditure should be directed wholly to increasing production, for example, by paying incentives to employers to offer increased employment and to workers to accept it, by establishing training arrangements and so on;

8 Existing expenditures on other things—ranging from defence to social services—should be kept at a stable level or reduced (although inflation might compel some adjustment upwards of, for example, social service payments);

9 The increased employment and production will—despite the tax concessions—result in increased tax revenue, probably very greatly increased revenue; this increase should be neutralised; government policy should aim at a considerable budget surplus, so as to prevent demand from increasing in step with employment and production and, if possible, to cut demand back below the levels which stimulated inflationary pressures;

10 Monetary policies, to be applied through the Central Bank and the trading bank system, should be directed to reinforcing the government's fiscal policies; in brief, it should aim at increasing production but it should do nothing avoidable— that is, nothing that is not an essential accompaniment of an increase in production and employment—to increase demand; funds should be made available on as liberal a basis as possible for expanded production—for establishment and equipping of new factories, for capital re-equipment of old ones, for capital investment for increased productivity of agriculture and the mineral industry; funds should be made available on much the same liberal basis to the construction industry but, although funds for private housing should not ordinarily be reduced, the demand for private housing should be kept under restraint until inflationary pressures have been relaxed;

11 Interest rates for production should be kept low; the incentive to productive investment should in that way be maximised; anti-inflationary policies might adopt a two-day movement of interest rates, making cheap money available for productive investment and relatively dear money available for consumption expenditure;

12 Thus, a two-tier interest-rate structure should be introduced, which will give greater flexibility to government policy at both the upper, inflationary and also the lower, deflationary level of the economy; at the upper, inflationary level of the economy, the interest rate for productive investment might be set at, say, 3 per cent or 4 per cent and the interest rate for consumption expenditure might be set at 8 per cent to 10 per cent; at the lower, deflationary level of the economy, the rate of interest for consumption expenditure might be brought right back to or below the level for productive investment;

13 As production increases and overtakes effective demand, inflationary pressures will slacken and government policies should then be moderated so that the economy does not build up into a crisis of over-production;

14 As inflationary pressures decline, the government should reduce its fiscal and monetary incentives so as to maintain a smooth equilibrium between production and demand; the easiest measures to modify quickly might be monetary

measures, including changes in one or both tiers in the two-tier interest-rate system, applied through the banking system; fiscal measures can only be applied more slowly and should be aimed at achieving smoothly any reduction in production and employment which may be necessary; any margin of production over demand might be accommodated by increased government expenditure at the appropriate moment;

15 The low point in production and employment in the economy should be clearly set at the full employment of all those people of working age who are self-supporting or supporting a family for a full working week (forty hours or whatever may be the accepted length);

16 Adjustments needed to maintain or restore equilibrium in the economy should be made above this basic full-employment level by expansion of production or by allowing production to fall towards its full-employment level; adjustment upwards should be by demand stimulation (that is, to move the economy out of actual or threatened deflation); adjustment downwards should be achieved by production stimulation (that is, to move the economy out of actual or threatened inflation);

17 Future government budgeting and national accounting should assess the aggregate production necessary to meet consumption and investment demand within the economy, to meet overseas commitments (including aid and defence commitments), to maintain full employment and to avoid unacceptable levels of inflation; policies should then be directed to achieving this production.

Habits and conventional wisdom have such power that policies adopted in accordance with the above will be questioned and sometimes opposed, even though they follow out, in some measure at least, trends which are already present in many of the mature developed economies. Trade-union support will be necessary if such policies are to succeed. So also will be the support of employers who will need to accustom themselves to the employment of new groups of people and perhaps also to the operation of their establishments for longer periods of time each day or each week.

The economy would operate at its highest level of production if all available labour were used for a maximum or 'optimum' working week all of the time. Indeed, the developed economies might gradually move towards this maximum level of production. The desire to do so will become more widespread if and when governments begin to implement policies aimed at increasing production as a counter to inflation. Once incentives for increased employment and production are given, there will probably be resistance to their removal when the need for them has passed. Consequently, there might be a gradual movement up towards a much less flexible employment and production ceiling, and governments might find themselves in almost as difficult a position to resist this as they have been in recent years to resist an increasingly tight definition of what constitutes full employment, and what interference with it is politically and socially acceptable.

This is possible. In fact, it is probable. Full employment will come to mean employment of everyone who wants to work for as long and as regularly as he wants to work. At that point, a good deal of flexibility will have gone out of government policies. But that point will, by any standards, take a fairly long time to reach. It might take as long as a generation and the available numbers of now unemployed or irregularly employed groups in the community might be constantly increasing. However, after a period of years which cannot now be forecast with any accuracy some other means will need to be found to maintain dynamism, with stability, in the economy. That is always the way: later solutions have to be found for later situations. But for now the solution to our problems of stability seems to lie in varying the level of production and employment, although always above what has so far been regarded as the full-employment level.

This means that governments, as well as the banking system when monetary measures are used, will have to make it clear that its stabilising stimuli to production are temporary and variable measures which will be removed and modified as circumstances change and may be reintroduced on a still later occasion when the present pressures have reappeared. Communities will need to be aware that groups of people will move into and then will move out of the market economy in accordance with the deliberate policies of the government. Individuals and groups such as trade unions and employers' associations will need to be aware of this and accept it.

Initially, at least, it seems likely that they will. They have accepted for a generation a situation in which workers who are supporting themselves or others are moved into and out of employment in accordance with the deliberate reflationary or deflationary policies of the government. If communities have accepted this, they are likely to accept movement into and out of the employed economy of people whose dependence on their paid employment or their additional paid employment is not primary but secondary. However, it has to be conceded—and it has been stressed elsewhere—that communities have become less and less prepared to accept a situation where primary bread-winners are moved periodically into and out of employment. After a time, these same communities, as we have already suggested above, will become accustomed to having opportunities for regular and continuous employment for everyone, even those who are not primary breadwinners, and resistance will develop to moving anyone periodically into or out of paid employment through deliberate government policies. That will come. But, in the meantime, governments will need to make clear to the communities for which they are responsible, the stabilising objectives which they have in mind, the consequent variability of their policies and the need to have flexibility and control of employment and production in the economy if full employment by our present standards, high gross national product by our present standards and a desirable outflow of aid and capital to poorer countries are to be achieved on a continuous basis.

That brings us to the third of those goals which we suggested at the beginning of this chapter could be achieved or promoted by the more intensive use of labour already available in the economy. We have shown, firstly, how more intensive use of this labour could expand production and income within the economy, and, secondly, how it could act as a short-term and long-term stabiliser of the economy. We now come to a consideration of the way in which more intensive use of available labour could help get more aid and capital to the developing countries and get it moving there more regularly and constantly.

The problem in the rich, developed countries supplying some of their surplus in aid to the poor, developing countries is that the rich have no surplus. The effective demand in the rich countries—for capital and consumer goods together—is so great that it takes up all or nearly all production. Sometimes it tries to take up more than the production available and inflation follows. But almost always effective demand is so close to aggregate production that an attempt to provide large-scale aid to developing countries (say, 1 per cent of gross national product, especially and to the extent that this is accompanied by other unrequited expenditures on defence, on outflow of private capital and so on), pushes this demand either into chasing imports, or into preserving for the domestic market goods which would otherwise have been exported, or into pushing up wages and prices in an inflationary spiral and so causing a further deterioration in the export/import situation. The net result will probably be a combination of all three of these effects.

In any event, there will be a deterioration in the balance of payments and reserves situation. Now, as we have seen, that deterioration cannot be redressed by seeking to make what amounts to a false or misleading reduction in effective demand, because production will probably decline faster so that there will be just as great or greater an imbalance at a lower level of employment. But it is possible to redress the deterioration in the payments balance by pushing up production while effective demand is kept at its existing level or is allowed to expand more slowly than production.

If, by the means we have just adumbrated, gross national product can be increased by 5 per cent, that is, $1 billion for a $20 billion economy, only half of that might be needed to restore balance between effective demand and supply in the domestic market—*provided* of course that demand is not allowed to move beyond existing levels. That means that $500 million is available for other purposes. Some or much of this might be used domestically. But some or much of it might be available also for investment in or aid to developing countries.

This will be especially the case according to the extent that the increased production provides substitutes for imports or releases goods from domestic consumption for export. To the further extent that it stabilises prices and improves the competitive position of domestic products *vis-à-vis* imports, it will also provide a disincentive to imports and an incentive to exports.

Much of the $500 million might therefore be available for investment in or aid to developing countries, while still keeping the international payments and reserves position in balance or even, as seems more likely, permitting their improvement.

Here then is a situation in which everyone seems to gain all round at the same time. If happiness consists in the improvement of the material position of the human animal—or if his happiness is promoted or made more attainable by an improvement in his material position—then the process which we have described would seem to be as ideally suited to the pursuit of human happiness everywhere as any that has yet been devised.

There is a question implicit in what we have just said. Will stabilisation of the economy through expansion of production enable each developed country to be more independent in its decisions about how much economic and technical aid it should give, how great an outflow of private capital it should allow? Or will each country need to take account of what its fellow developed countries are doing? Will it face a drain on its reserves and the threat of insolvency if it does not? Will that drain or that threat start immediately, or will it come along only some time later?

At the moment, the developed countries have only a limited degree of independence. Those countries which give a lot of aid and allow a substantial net outflow of private capital and generally make large unrequited outlays—countries like the United States and Britain—have had their international reserves seriously run down and often look—although it will never happen—as though they are insolvent or about to become so. Those countries like Japan and Germany whose aid and capital outflow and, generally, unrequited outlays are relatively small have large and growing reserves and look as though insolvency is as remote as it well could be. Of course, as we have seen, the cause of the difficulties of Britain and the United States is the *total* of their non-economic outlays; the robustness of Japan and Germany can be traced to the relative *smallness* of their *total* non-economic outlays.

But the evidence is that these non-economic outlays can be maintained, if they can be maintained at all, only by a sharing of non-economic outlays by all of the developed countries together.

In September 1968, Mr Robert Roosa, who had shortly before been Secretary of the United States Treasury, put forward publicly a proposal for evening out the impact of capital flows on payments equilibria of developed countries in a way which would help to mobilise more funds for the developing countries. He suggested that a group of developed countries should combine to make a joint commitment of funds for several years at a time to the various established international banks for development, the contributions of individual members of the consortium—but not the total of their joint commitment—being adjusted year by year as they ran surpluses or deficits in their other international transactions. Mr Roosa said that, if this smacked of 'pie in the sky', so, twenty years ago, did 'much of what we are eating now'.

Despite a good deal of consultation among the developed countries, especially within the Organisation for Economic Cooperation and Development, both before and since Mr Roosa put forward his proposal, not a great deal has been done to harmonise aid contributions to take account of different and changing balance-of-payments situations. Although some governments increased their aid, this was only a little more than sufficient to make up, in monetary terms, for the failure of United States government aid to increase and its ultimate decline, even in monetary terms, during the 1960's. The flow of government aid of all the developed countries combined to developing countries which had already surpassed $6 billion in 1961, had slipped back to $6 billion in 1964 and had moved up to only $6.9 billion in 1968. In real terms, there had been a substantial decline in aggregate aid.

Even if aid contributions had been more convincingly harmonised, that would have dealt with only a part—for some countries, a fairly small part—of total non-economic outlays. Mr Roosa's proposal contemplated evening out only a part of aid flows to the developing countries. The chances of going beyond this and sharing among the developed countries, on some sort of agreed equitable basis, the total of non-economic outlays, covering political and strategic as well as aid expenditures, must be regarded as remote; not only are the economic difficulties formidable but the political impediments must be pretty nearly insuperable. But, in any event, what is clear is that, whatever the will of individual governments at the moment, they cannot give as much economic aid or allow as much private investment in developing countries as the latter need, or as the developed countries themselves would like to give. They cannot act independently or they will risk economic disaster independently. And they cannot act in unison because the political and economic difficulties are too formidable to allow it.

Will stabilisation of the economy through upward movement of production change all this? To an important extent, it will. Governments will, initially at least, have a larger margin of external resources with which they will be able to make grants or extend credits. This will be a normal, traditional way of disposing of surplus production on world 'markets' and of using available international reserves. So long as, for example, Britain and the United States have reserves available for aid, it will be of no immediate consequence to their own aid programmes whether or not other developed countries have these reserves too.

But pressures are likely gradually to build up. Those countries which have become used to a world role will probably resume such a role when they again have the resources available to sustain it. Those countries which have avoided a world role will probably continue to avoid it, although there are signs that Japan, at least, might gradually assume greater responsibilities—political and strategic, as well as economic—in her part of the world.

In these circumstances, the new policies of stabilisation through expansion of production will mean only that the margins for aid and capital outflow will be larger and that each developed country will be able *independently* to sustain these expenditures for a longer time. However, if they are to be sustained at the ever-increasing levels which would seem to be necessary, for an indefinitely continuing period, harmonisation of policies among the developed countries—or at least among the major developed countries—would seem still to be necessary in the longer term.

The more intensive use of labour resources—principally of labour now in use but also of other labour potential—already existing within the economy will then achieve these three goals. Firstly, it will expand production in absolute terms and thus increase the gross national product and average per capita income; secondly, it will provide a means which has so far eluded the policy-makers, of stabilising the economy at the upper, inflationary level of the economy; and, thirdly, it will enable the developed economies more readily to permit the outflow of substantial economic and technical aid and private capital which is necessary for the economic development of the poorer countries (although it will still not permit an unlimited outflow of these funds, and certainly not an outflow limited only by increases in gross national product).

This more intensive use of labour resources is not only revolutionary in its effects but is also based on a theory which is revolutionary in terms of modern economic thought. It does not only modify the modern application of Keynesian theory; it provides a new theory of Keynesian equilibrium which will have far-reaching implications both for the rich, advanced sophisticated economies themselves and for their relationships with their poorer, more primitive fellows. Since this theory can be the basis and the origin of so many changed economic attitudes and economic effects—and can so dramatically change the economic and social context in which people will conduct their lives—we may perhaps recapitulate the essence of that theory again. Especially would it seem to be of value here to offer this recapitulation in terms of the differences between the new theory and the old theory on which economic policy and practice have been based up until now under a Keynesian system.

When these differences are put forward, it may seem that the differences between the old and the new theories are not great. In fact, the new theory, if valid, will have far-reaching economic effects and there will also flow from it a series of political repercussions which could have a major effect on the foreign policies, as well as the economic policies, of some at least of the major powers and could introduce a new element into a wide range of political relationships. The policies of the United States and Britain could, in particular, undergo fundamental and dramatic changes, and their relationships, not only with the developing countries, but also with such friends as Japan and with such competitors as the USSR, could be dramatically different in the future from what they have been in the past.

With that as background, let us briefly recapitulate the new theory in a way which relates it especially to the theory—and the policy and practice—of the past.

At the upper employment level of the economy, when serious inflationary strains begin to appear, the primary preoccupation should be to move production up to higher levels so that supply will be brought into equilibrium with, and gradually edge beyond demand. When the economy has moved down and when strains begin to appear in the other direction, that is, when serious deflationary strains and a more than acceptable level of unemployment appear or threaten, the principal preoccupation should be with demand, and the effort should be to move demand up until it is in harmony with the level of supply at an acceptable level of employment.

This does not ignore the possibility—and indeed the desirability—of a secondary preoccupation. At the upper employment level, this secondary preoccupation will be with demand. If the economy is to be stabilised, it will be important, not only that production be moved up, but also that demand either (i) be moved down or (ii) be maintained at the existing level or (iii) in any event, be allowed to move up at a lesser rate than the acceleration in production. Again, at the lower employment level, it is important not only that demand be moved up but also that production be allowed to move up, although—for best results in most circumstances—not at such a rate that it outstrips the acceleration in demand and thus causes the accumulation of inventories and loss of confidence.

But the primary preoccupation must be to move up production at the upper level of employment of the economy and to move up demand at the lower level of employment of the economy. This is very different from the present approach.

At the upper level of the economy, present policies seek to establish an equilibrium *downwards*, by bringing demand down to the level of supply. The much more positive and beneficial approach—beneficial to the individual producer and consumer and the economy as a whole—is to seek an equilibrium *upwards*, that is, to push supply (in effect, to push production) up to the level of existing demand. If production goes up beyond demand so that a new deflationary disequilibrium occurs, then the correct approach seems to be to allow production to slide down—but to maintain demand so as to ensure that the economy still operates at a very high level. This very high level of operation would, under the new proposed arrangements for more intensive use of labour in the economy, be at least the level implied by the economy running at *full employment as we understand it at the moment.*

As contrasted with the new theory, the present policy and practice mean that our primary preoccupation is with demand at both the upper and the lower levels of employment of the economy. When the economy is moving into an inflationary disequilibrium, our policy-makers at present seek to damp down demand. When the economy is moving into a deflationary dis-equilibrium, our present policy-makers seek to stimulate demand.

There are, admittedly, differing approaches to the way in which particular economists advocate that demand should be stimulated or depressed. The two major approaches are the monetary and the fiscal. Legions of economists and administrators line them-selves up behind the splendid standards of monetary control. At the head of the monetarists stand formidable figures like Milton Friedman. But legions no less numerous and no less formidable form up behind the banner of fiscal control and have equally celebrated intellectuals as their highly honoured leaders.

But the primary preoccupation of both groups is with demand at both the upper and the lower levels of employment of the economy. It is this immutable preoccupation which has led them both into error. It is this primary preoccupation with its resultant error which has made it so difficult to maintain stability in individual national economies, and which has made it well-nigh impossible to maintain stability in all of the highly developed economies at the one time, and to maintain equilibrium in the developed countries while they pursue policies of substantial aid to developing countries, along with other large non-economic outlays. The new theory should remove this error. In so doing, it should produce a lot of the stability which is now lacking. What we need is a new style of thinking. We need to adopt an attitude that an economy suffering from inflation cannot afford not to have maximum production; cannot afford to have people idle who can, by one means or another, be drawn into market production; cannot afford to pay out social services, without any requital in production, except where this is unavoidable or would be in-equitable. What our economic policies do now is to act as though we can afford these things. In fact, the only time an economy can 'afford' to hand out social service payments—unrequited social service payments—which it doesn't have to hand out, is during a depression or a recession or a deflation, when the object is to get the economy moving again by boosting demand in relation to supply.

When the economy gets into a situation of inflation, our present policies absurdly *cut* production; they *cut* employment; they put out of production and employment hundreds of thousands and even millions of people, depending on the size of the economy, who have been contributing and still could contribute massively to gross national product and national income; and they pay out vast amounts of money in unemployment benefits to these people to keep them out of production.

This is as massive an absurdity as the policies of the 1930's which, in the name of setting the economy to rights, directed themselves to intensifying the weakness of demand which had been the cause of the depression in the first place. This absurdity of the 1960's and 1970's—just like the absurdity of the 1930's—must cease.

X
Transfers of Labour

We have hypothesised that, within the context of a buoyant demand, the stability and dynamism of a modern economy will be promoted by the more intensive use of labour within the economy in order to expand production. The same result can be, and has been, achieved by immigration of labour from abroad; or an economy can be depressed by a chronic net emigration of labour. Both the more intensive use of labour within the economy —defined most obviously as an increase in the total body of labour through performance of more work by those in employment and employment of previously unemployed groups—and the immigration of labour add to the numbers in the work-force.

But there is another means by which effective labour and thus production can be increased. Most labour can be used in a number of ways. It can work with other less efficient or more efficient factors of production. It can be skilled or unskilled. It might use the skills which it has acquired or of which it is capable, or it might not. If labour can be transferred from a less efficient to a more efficient use, then the total labour resources— the productivity of labour and aggregate production—will be increased. If an economy has factors of production which make it more efficient in the provision of certain services, then—up to a point at least—it will maximise production if labour is transferred to these service industries. Equally, there are some countries so placed that their labour can be more productively used in secondary—manufacturing—industries and still others best placed, through a bounty of land and climate, to grow food, raise livestock and plant forests. Labour transfers to achieve the most efficient combination of factors of production will increase labour resources, add to production and, although it is not by itself a total solution, contribute to the dynamism and stability of the economy.

While the now developed countries were industrialising—during the nineteenth and early twentieth centuries—they needed markets outside their own frontiers.[1] They needed these markets even when their economies were at full stretch, because the productivity of workers, who formed the bulk of the population, was generally greater than the demand they were able to exert; but, with even greater urgency, they needed these markets especially so long as cyclical downturns were an actuality or a prospect. The gathering strength of the industrial community, and the passing of political power to it, induced governments to seek out means which would help to secure markets for their industries outside their own economic frontiers. Consequently, they negotiated trade agreements. They obtained entry for their manufactures into foreign markets on assured or more nearly assured terms through these agreements. In return, they had to make concessions in their own markets; otherwise no real negotiation, which implies a prospect of reasonably balanced concessions by both sides, and no mutually beneficial agreement, would have been possible. Where negotiations and agreements were between countries both of which were industrialising, these concessions could be wholly or primarily confined to industrial items: there could be a mutually beneficial penetration of each other's markets, perhaps allowing one country to concentrate on certain industrial products for the enlarged market, while the second could devote itself more fully to other items for the same enlarged market.

---

[1] In just the same way as developing countries today need markets for their manufactures outside their own economies. 'If the less developed countries are to industrialise, they must be able from an early stage to sell their manufactured goods. In many cases the domestic market cannot absorb them, and they can only be made if they can be sold abroad. . . . India cannot (manufacture transistor radios) unless she can export them: Indians cannot afford them' (Michael Stewart, *Keynes and After*, Penguin Books Ltd [Pelican original], 1967, p. 233).

Where the negotiations and agreements were between an industrialising country and a primary-exporting country another form of balanced concessions had to be realised. Access for manufactures had to be paid for by access for farm, livestock and other primary products. This meant that agriculture in the industrialising countries had to meet the competition of imports from overseas. The manufacturers got the benefit of an overseas market; and the farmers in the industrialising country paid the price for it. In some cases—a limited number, of which the outstanding case was Britain—this might result in free trade or a high degree of free trade. In others, the protection given to the agriculture of the industrialising countries was negotiated downwards in order to win access for the expanding production of their industrial economy.

If this process of negotiation led ultimately to completely free access for primary commodities into the industrialising country, the farmers and other primary producers in the industrialising country stood or fell solely according to their competitive efficiency. If the grain farmers of Britain could compete freely with the grain farmers of the prairies, they survived. If not or to the extent that they could not, they were swept away. Free access of this kind was realised only rarely and infrequently. But the movement by negotiation of most of the industrialising countries was in the direction of liberal access for primary products. The industrialising countries had to be willing to modify their protection for their own agriculture if they were to negotiate meaningfully for markets in the non-industrialising countries.

There was another factor. High costs of food would push up the costs of industrial production. If some industrialising countries protected their agriculture more than others, the export costs of their manufactures might become so high as to damage their competitive position. In a highly competitive, unstable industrial market, in which production tended chronically to outrun effective demand and which was subject to wide fluctuations through cyclical disturbances, any increase in the cost structure could jeopardise the industrialising process. It could cause shrinkage in the already comparatively small domestic market for manufacturers; it could destroy export markets, except where they could be absolutely secured as colonial possessions; it could halt or retard further investment in manufacturing industry; and it could cause political and social disorders, because of the damage done both to the new entrepreneurial class and to the newly swollen ranks of urban, mainly industrial labour.

The last point is crucial. As the industrialising process continued, political power gradually passed from landed to industrial interests. These industrial interests formed governments and determined policies. Their needs became paramount both in matters of domestic concern and in relations with other countries. They needed markets for their manufactures. So they had to negotiate with other governments to win these markets. In doing so, they could not avoid agreeing that they would limit the protection which they would give to their own domestic agriculture, and so expand access for the foreigner with whom they were negotiating. The industrialist increasingly held political power and he made the bargain that suited him.

Domestic agricultural interests could and did battle to safeguard their position, and they never completely lost political and social power. Consequently, a struggle persisted between industrial and agricultural interests in the industrialising countries, a struggle which was not resolved in precisely the same way in each. The struggle established some sort of equilibrium, changing from time to time; and some sort of equilibrium, once again changing over time, was also achieved between the industrialising and the primary-exporting countries.

While the equilibrium between domestic agricultural and industrial interests and between 'agricultural' and 'industrial' countries was never perfect and did not persist unchanged for long periods, it nevertheless had a high practical value. The two sides domestically and the two sides externally each had sufficient relative power to force a balance. Industrial interests could not —generally—ride rough-shod over agricultural interests or vice versa. Industrialising countries—unless they secured their markets through colonisation—had an interest in striking a bargain with agricultural countries; they could neither dominate nor ignore those countries which had not yet started or gone far in the industrialising process. The balance always tended to favour the 'comers' rather than those whose greatest period lay in the past; but it was a reasonable balance nevertheless. Sometimes, indeed,

some of the agricultural countries supplying rapidly industrialising countries in boom periods, made large gains and their
people achieved a very high standard of living. It was an unstable affluence; but it was good while it lasted.

Keynesian economic policies changed all this. Gradually, since
the end of the Second World War, the balance between domestic
agriculture and secondary industry, and between industrial and
agricultural countries, has disappeared. It has not been deliberately destroyed; it has not gone because of any clear-cut acts of
policy aimed explicitly at removing the earlier equilibria. It has
just disappeared under the influence of much wider policies
which have made these equilibria irrelevant. No one in the industrialised countries has sought to maintain them because no one
in those countries has seen his interests to lie—or lie sufficiently
—in maintaining them. And, much as they might have wanted
to, no one in the agricultural, primary-exporting countries has
had the power to maintain these equilibria which once were and
could be again so important to the developing countries.

The cause has been the high and relatively stable economic
growth in the developed countries, the increasing affluence of
the average consumer, the consequently predominating importance of the domestic market to the industrial producer and,
beyond that, the importance of other *developed*, secondary-
industry-producing-and-exporting-country markets. Almost everyone else gets ignored. That means mainly that the primary
producer, and exporter, in terms of a negotiated equilibrium,
gets ignored.

In this situation, the great determinant has been the Keynesian
economy's virtue of stability. Reliability—quite apart from volume
and growth—lies with the markets of the highly developed,
Keynesian-controlled industrialised countries. Unreliability—as
well as small volume and slow or negative growth—lies with the
markets of the primary exporting (generally developing) countries. To attach export trade too much to these latter countries
could therefore be to import instability. To say that this instability
is largely a result of factors—unsatisfactory terms of trade and
violent fluctuations in commodity prices—originating in the
highly industrialised countries may make this attitude to trade
with the primary-exporting countries seem unjust; but it does

not alter the facts of the situation. The development of trade must be, above all, a practical matter which pays close regard to economic facts. Humanitarian objectives, the traders would say, are generally for consideration in other than trade contexts; they should be kept separate from the hard bargaining of the trading and financial world.

In this situation, the highly industrialised countries have lost their need and their economic incentive to negotiate trade agreements with their primary-producing fellows. Especially in so far as the latter are also developing countries, the developed countries now have, if anything, a disincentive to such negotiations. They have no need to make concessions for access to their own agricultural market in order to win markets for their industry in primary-exporting countries because those markets are quite simply not of sufficient consequence to them. As a result, the pressure for protection by agricultural interests in the highly industrialised countries is afforded an opportunity to become much more effective. There is no effective opposition—and sometimes not even token opposition—to it from industry. Industry is so strong that it feels it can support a highly protected agriculture; and the community as a whole, including secondary and tertiary industries, feels a responsibility to do so since the economy as a whole is dynamic, whereas agriculture, although often dynamic in the sense of increase in productivity, is undynamic in terms of the relation between supply and effective demand. Finally, the danger that one country will lose its competitive position because of high costs compared with other highly industrialised countries, loses much or all of its force when all these countries behave towards their domestic agriculture in much the same way.

Therefore, genuine negotiation between the industrialising and the primary-exporting (generally developing) countries virtually ceases. What happens instead is that a number of essentially unilateral expedients are embarked upon. In the case of tropical products, for example, revenue duties might be imposed for fiscal reasons by the temperate developed countries and might be unilaterally removed as a gesture of aid and goodwill to the developing countries. By and large, tropical products do not compete with the temperate agricultural products of the advanced countries, and therefore protective duties are irrelevant. When a tropical product does compete—for example, tropical cane sugar with temperate beet sugar—the European domestic producer insists on his protection and there is little hope of negotiating it downwards. Some products, such as wool, though temperate products, are not produced in anything like sufficient volume or quality to meet the needs of the developed economies.[2] Consequently, wool gets easy access to the markets of most of the developed countries. Access is not negotiated or granted for any reasons of aid or goodwill. It is unilaterally allowed because there is no strong argument for protection, and free, or at least easy access, carries with it advantages to the importing, developed country, for example, for its textile industry and its consumers.

Beyond that, it is usually a question of just how far any developed country is prepared to go in granting access to primary products. It is not compelled, for economic reasons, to *negotiate* access at all. It might feel persuaded, for political and humanitarian reasons, to *grant* access to primary-exporting, developing countries as a form of economic aid, unilaterally determined and unilaterally granted. Not surprisingly, each country will choose to give access to those commodities which will do least or no harm to its domestic production. Voluntarily to aid someone else by doing damage to a politically significant sector of the domestic electorate is seldom likely to make much sense, and seldom does. Therefore, if a developed country wants to give access to the agriculture of developing countries, it will do so in a way which will leave domestic agriculture untouched.

All of this suggests that, not only will agriculture in the industrialised countries not be negotiated away, but, on the contrary, agricultural protection might well be intensified as time goes on, if only to ensure that farm incomes keep more or less in step— or not too outrageously out of step—with the forward march of industrial and tertiary incomes.

Some of the old pressures for transfer of labour from agriculture to secondary and tertiary industry have therefore disappeared. Transfers have indeed taken place and continue to take place in the developed countries—as also in the developing countries. The

---

[2] This does not apply to production of and demand for wool in the United States. United States sheep growers produce a lot of wool and get a lot of protection.

recent development of high-yielding 'super-seeds', the use of fertilisers and the resultant Green Revolution in some of the developing countries have brought such profits to some of the land-owners (for example, in Pakistan) that they have been able to buy tractors and other farm machinery and thus dismiss much of their farm labour and resume land which they had formerly let to tenant-farmers.[3] The labour thus released has been flooding into the cities in search of other, non-agricultural employment. Many millions of people in such countries as India and Pakistan are likely to be transferred from the farms to the cities under the pressure of these economic forces in the next ten or fifteen years.

In Iran, there has been a similar relative movement of population from the countryside to the towns. During the decade of the 1960's, the population of the countryside increased by only 18 per cent, whereas the population of Teheran increased by 81 per cent, of medium towns by 49 per cent and of small towns by 55 per cent. The difference between Iran and many other developing countries was that the people who came from the countryside were readily able to find employment in the secondary and service industries of the towns, especially Teheran, so that the growth of shanty towns of landless peasants has not been a characteristic of Iran's recent growth.

Much the same sort of thing—although there have obviously been variations in points of detail—has happened in the developed countries in recent years. It would be quite wrong to suggest that the diminishing need to subject domestic agriculture to external competition has maintained the level of the labour force in agriculture. It hasn't. And, in the future, industry might still be able to draw substantial amounts of labour away from agriculture. Almost certainly, it will. The trend is already well-established. Productivity in agriculture in Europe has increased so much since the end of the Second World War that a vastly increased production is being obtained, through much higher capitalisation in equipment and use of fertilisers, from a much

[3] The net effect on farm and village labour will vary with locality and other circumstances. Mechanisation—often perhaps unnecessary—will reduce the need for direct farm labour but multiple cropping and the expansion of demand for local services will tend to increase the aggregate demand for direct labour on the farms and indirect labour in the villages.

reduced labour force. This trend has been, and will continue to be, assisted by the ease with which displaced labour can find employment in the cities; and it is reinforced to the extent that discontented farm labour seeks out the better living conditions and higher wages of the cities. But, although there will always tend to be a surplus of population in the countryside, arising from natural increase, which will find its way to the cities, the transfer of labour otherwise from agriculture to industry cannot go on indefinitely. Agriculture cannot be operated wholly with machines; someone must remain even if only to look after the machines. All that we can say is that some further reduction of the farm population can still be achieved without necessarily reducing total agricultural output.

What will happen then? It may be that pressure by the agricultural sector to maintain protection will diminish; or it will lose a considerable amount of its force. The farm vote has so far been important to political parties; if the numbers engaged in farming greatly diminish, then the farm vote will be much less important. But will it ever diminish so much in size and importance that protection will be greatly reduced or discarded? Even if the farm vote can be ignored, will it be in the 'national interest' to abandon agriculture? Does some sort of 'territorial imperative' operate in favour of use of agricultural land? Will there ever be sufficient organised pressure from industry or from consumers or others to cause agricultural protection to be severely reduced? We cannot answer all these questions but the answer is sufficiently uncertain to compel us to put a query against the prospect that agricultural production in the industrialised countries will ever be much less than it is today, and that transfers of labour to industry will ever be larger than would permit continuing agricultural production at about its present level.

Even so, industry will continue to draw off some labour from agriculture; and economic growth in the industrialised countries is likely, for some years to come, to be helped by an infusion of agricultural labour into industry. And, after that period, will be helped by movement of surplus population arising from natural increase from the countryside to the cities.

Is economic growth in the industrialised countries likely to be helped by any other similar transfers of labour? Here the answer must be much less certain. It could happen. The atmosphere in industry is such that there is no overwhelming reason why it should not happen. Transfers from one industry to another are much easier when the economy is at or near full stretch and growth rates are high. The relative decline of some industries while other new industries have been undergoing hectic expansion has been a feature of the post-war experience. Is it possible that the industrialised countries will gradually concentrate more of their resources on the more sophisticated industries and move out of those industries where their marginal efficiency is lowest? It is possible, and already some indicators suggest that they might be willing to move in this direction. If they did, they could transfer resources in a way which would help them to maintain growth rates; and it would introduce certain changes in the relations between the industrialised and the developing countries.

Let us examine more closely this possible change in the production and trade relationship between the developed and the developing countries. At present, the developed countries are, generally, faced with labour shortage. The developing countries are, generally, faced with massive and increasing labour surplus. The pull of economic forces is to transfer the surplus of labour in the developing countries to meet the shortage of labour in the developed countries. This potential pull of economic forces was given concrete exemplification in the migration, for example, of West Indians and others to Britain and of Mexicans to the United States.

This movement, although it seems superficially to be towards an equilibrium position at which demand for labour would be equalled by supply of labour, would in fact maintain and accelerate growth in the developed world and itself create a further demand for labour. The process would be continuous, unless the governments in the countries receiving the immigrants applied policies to halt or retard it. This is what we have explained earlier, for example, in dealing with the 'gold-rush effect'. We have also explained that, if this 'gold-rush effect' is reversed, and an immigrant inflow is replaced by an outward movement of labour from the developed country, production and investment in that country will tend to fall and the downward process will, in its turn, tend to be continuous also. One of the important factors in establishing a dynamic equilibrium—the expression is not internally contradictory—is that the supply of labour should be constant or increasing.

The natural pull of economic forces on labour can be satisfied in two major ways: either by movement of labour to the industrial centres or by movement of industrial activity to the areas where surplus labour exists. This latter possibility provides a potential solution to the current disequilibrium and offers some chance of reversing the gold-rush effect caused by dynamism in the developed world, with its concurrent result of increasing even more rapidly the gap between living standards of the richer and the poorer countries, and—much more importantly—of leaving an insufficient stimulus to improvements in production and productivity in the developing countries.

A great deal of attention is given to the gap in living standards between rich and poor; and a great deal of emotion goes into statements about how this gap should be bridged. Much of this is wasted. For most developing countries, the gap is going to get wider for at least a generation yet,[4] no matter what happens. The average individual in the United States in 2000 AD is going to be richer than the average individual in Chad in 2000 AD by much more than he is today. This could be changed if Chad is discovered to be sitting on a treasure-chest of gold or a vast barrel of oil; or it could be changed if a monstrous catastrophe—say, a nuclear war—devastated the United States. But, in ordinary circumstances, the gap will be greater in 2000 AD than it is now; and no one would seriously want it to be otherwise. No sensible person would want to reduce income in the United States simply in order that the gap should be closed a little and the people of the United States brought a little closer to the poverty which afflicts other people.

Rather the important thing is that absolute living standards in

---

[4] In any reasonably foreseeable circumstances, the 'gap' is likely to take much more than a generation to close. If we take, first, an advanced country with a per capita GNP of $2,000 growing at a real rate of only 2% per annum (and most developed countries are growing much faster than this) and, second, a developing country with a per capita GNP of $200 and growing at 4% (which is optimistic, especially in the context of rapid population growth), then it would take 85 years before the gap, then grown to over $5,000, would begin to narrow and 120 years before the gap would be closed (at a per capita income of $21,000).

the developing countries should be moved up. They should be better off, even though the rich countries might, in the meantime, be better off still. It is possible for the developing countries at the present time to aspire to riches not because the developed world is poor but because it is—by the standards of all previous human history—immensely rich. Provided appropriate policies are adopted by the developed countries—for example, policies of the kind we have adumbrated earlier—the developing countries will be ever more able realistically to aspire to riches, the more immensely rich the developed countries become.

One means of moving up production and income and living standards is to establish new industries in the developing world or to expand existing industries. This could be done, *inter alia*, by establishing industry where there is surplus labour. An artificial decentralisation of industry has never been easy—even within a national economy. International decentralisation might seem to carry with it even more difficulties. But it also has some advantages. One of them is that the more or less uniform remuneration of labour within a national economy does not apply internationally.

How can industrial activity be moved to the areas where surplus labour exists?

It would be logical for those industries requiring a high proportion of labour and a low proportion of skills and/or capital to be established in the developing countries. These industries would be especially such things as textiles and the processing industries. On the latter, it seems particularly irrational that unprocessed food and raw materials should be imported into the highly developed countries when the relatively simple tasks of transformation can be equally well, and perhaps more cheaply, performed in the countries of origin. Supplies must be assured; and the developed countries might be hesitant to abandon certain industries until they have this assurance. But the need for assurance about supplies is just about as great for the unprocessed as it is for the processed product. The variety of sources of supply is or could quickly become just as great, so that if some threat developed to supply of some processed commodity from, say, Africa or Latin America, alternative sources would be readily available in, say, Asia and Australasia.

The opposition to reduction or abandonment of the processing industries in the developed countries has, in the past, not really been based on the need to safeguard supplies, but on the desire to protect local industries. This has perhaps been particularly true of such countries as Italy which, though highly developed, have had backward areas and have moved to a state of dynamic growth and full employment on a national scale only comparatively recently. They have not been prepared, therefore, to give up or reduce any of their industries without good cause—and good cause has usually meant striking the perfectly reasonable bargain that they get more benefit for their industries than they give up. As we have suggested earlier, the developing countries are usually just not in a position to offer this sort of bargain and they are the ones which usually have the greatest interest in removing or reducing protection for the processing industries.

So these industries continue. But they are not necessarily of continuing advantage to the developed economies. As we have already hypothesised, labour is a valuable commodity and might be the most important element in the future dynamism of the developed countries. To use it needlessly in processing industries might consequently mean the surrender of easily obtainable accretions to gross national product and per capita income. To transfer labour from these industries to industries where its product will be greater will win these accretions to GNP and per capita income, and also contribute to the economic development and to increases in the GNP and per capita income of the developing countries. Just how much labour could be transferred in this way both within the developed countries and between the developing and the developed countries is hard to calculate but it could be enough to make a sizeable contribution to growth in both groups of countries.

Much the same might be said about textiles and other labour-intensive industries.

Some companies in the developed countries have already established manufacturing plants in Asian, African and other relatively cheap labour countries in order to avoid the high and rapidly increasing costs of labour at home. Often these are joint projects, in which the company enters into some arrangement with the government or a company of the developing country to operate the plant jointly and share the profits, perhaps over an agreed period of years. This is likely to continue and could contribute to increases in GNP in both the developed and the developing countries.

But will arrangements go beyond this and allow the transfer of whole industries to the developing countries? The industry which has most often been designated for advantageous transfer is textiles. Many people have considered the possibility of transferring textile production to the developing countries and, in recent years, it has become one of the preoccupations of the United Nations Conference on Trade and Development. In 1970, French economist Jacques de Bandt placed a report before UNCTAD which argued in favour of expansion of textile industries in developing countries and free entry for their textile products into the developed markets, even though this might mean that the rich, advanced countries might have to reconstruct and perhaps abandon their own textile industries.

Others have put forward arguments against de Bandt's thesis. They have said that textiles is not such a labour-intensive industry as many people think. The Organisation for European Co-operation and Development has calculated that, whereas it cost between $6000 and $10,000 to create a new job in a spinning mill in 1945, now it costs $50,000 to $100,000. Technological developments have already introduced automatic spinning mills in the United States and Japan. Not much labour would be used with these plants in developing countries, therefore, and highly skilled people would be needed to look after the complex and costly equipment. Other arguments against too facile an acceptance of mass transfer of textile production to the developing countries are that textile production is best located near the big consumer markets and must be closely related to fashions in these markets; that the developing countries should not gamble too much of their future on textiles, which has historically been an unstable industry; that it would be unrealistic to expect that technological progress in the textiles industry could be stopped so that the cheap-labour advantages of the developing countries can be maintained; and that the raw materials for textiles are now derived largely from the developed countries in the form of synthetic fibres, rather than from the developing countries in the form of cotton, wool, silk, and so on.

But even if the economic arguments for transfer of textiles to the developing countries were unassailable, would the governments of developed countries allow it? The evidence is that when Japanese or other textiles threaten the textiles industry of the United States or Western European countries, protection is thrown up against the inflow of imports. Some imports are permitted and even some regular increase; but too great an increase provokes a protective reaction. This reaction is rather like developed governments' reaction in favour of protection for their own agriculture. It is estimated that there are about 1 million textiles workers in the United States, more than half a million in Germany and about half a million in France. Why should the governments of these countries set the livelihood of all these people at risk for the sake of developing countries which can offer them no negotiated economic advantage in return?

What will happen, therefore, is that there will probably be a gradual increase in exports of textiles and other relatively labour-intensive products from the developing to the developed countries and thus a gradual transfer of these industries to the former. However, like agriculture, substantial production in labour-intensive or relatively labour-intensive industries will probably be maintained in the developed countries, especially where these industries have been traditionally large employers of labour and, probably of lesser significance, of capital.

In other words—and this will surprise no one—there are inhibiting factors against unlimited progress along this road of labour-transfers. These inhibiting factors are not necessarily economic; in fact, most of them will certainly not be economic. The developed countries will rather see social, political and strategic factors as operating against too complete a co-ordination —or, as they might see it, a fragmentation—of production between their home economies and economies of uncertain stability scattered all round the world. But greater movement than has been made already can be achieved in transfers of labour, without creating anxieties of a magnitude which will make governments exercise restraints. The important thing is not so much that the transition to a perfect division of labour—perfect by economic criteria—should be made quickly and completely; rather the important thing is that as much movement should be made as is realistic politically, socially and strategically. A first policy stage might be to reduce protection for simple, labour-intensive industries in the developed countries. A second stage might be to impose disincentives for the operation of these industries in the developed countries so that the transfer of capital and labour to more sophisticated industrial sectors will stimulate the rate of national economic growth.

Some industries will quickly identify themselves or—as in the case of textiles—seem perhaps misleadingly to identify themselves as suitable for this transition. Others will become apparent as time passes and as a new pattern of production and trade emerges. What will be necessary at the outset is a mode of thinking which will look towards transfer of resources from industries suited to the labour-surplus in developing countries to industries in which the marginal efficiency of the developed economies is greatest. However, there are two questions which must be asked. The first is what is the incentive of the developed countries to abandon certain industries: is it a unilateral concession or is it something which is necessary, economically, to themselves? The second question is how will this concession work out in practice in affecting the relations between the developing and the developed countries?

XI
The Implications of a New Pattern of Production

Why should the developed countries abandon certain industries? One reason has already been given: developed countries are likely more easily to be able to maintain a high growth rate if they move resources to industries in which their comparative advantage is greatest. But there is another reason, not unlinked with the first, but also distinct from it. It is that circumstances may already be developing, because of population trends, which will make it, not merely desirable to draw developing countries more fully into production to keep growth rates high, but that this may be essential if real growth is to be kept above the rate of technological advance.

If population is little better than static and fully-employed, growth will depend only on improvements in productivity. At any given point of time, these improvements will be greater in some industries than others. In some industries, especially the older ones, productivity may remain relatively or absolutely static over long periods of time. A substantial improvement in productivity in one or a few industries might, when spread over the whole economy, mean only a very modest rate of economic growth.

Other things will then follow. If the rate of growth is low, the incentive to investment will be low. The opposite of the 'gold-rush' effect will take place. When certain elements tend to move the economy forward, they tend to spark off dynamism elsewhere and so there is a 'multiplier' or 'circular causation' effect. When certain elements tend to move the economy downwards, the multiplier or circular causation effect will tend to accentuate this downward trend. If the rate of growth declines, the factors which caused this decline will operate to cause a further decline. The rate of growth may become zero or negative even though, with a static population, technical capacity exists to maintain a positive rate. Further, although fiscal and other measures might succeed in maintaining full employment, the rate of real economic growth might be small, zero or negative, unless transfers of labour take place to the more efficient industries where productivity is increasing.

There is another problem which may be exemplified by agriculture. In recent years, agricultural productivity has increased and there have been transfers of labour from agriculture to industry. Both of these developments should mean an increase in real economic growth and to some extent both of them do. However, the real increase in economic growth is, in some cases, less than appears. The transfer of agricultural labour, in so far as it is fully employed elsewhere, is an unmitigated gain in production. But the increased productivity of the labour force remaining in agriculture may result in an increased production which cannot be wholly absorbed by the market. The result is that surpluses are created, market prices tend to fall, protective devices are established and world resources which are more efficient for agricultural production are left underutilised while less efficient resources are overutilised. In a situation where economic growth is rapid for other reasons—for example, through the drawing of new labour into the economy—this arrangement is tolerable. But it will become less tolerable if and when growth rates start to decline and cannot readily be sustained by means other than the transfer of labour to the more highly productive industries and the use of labour for production which is in greatest demand on the market.

The outlines of the emergent situation must remain vague. However, one possible prospect is that, in order to maintain a fairly high rate of economic growth, the developed countries will want to move out of the industries in which increases in productivity are lowest and into those industries where increases in productivity are highest. The former industries—presumably labour-intensive industries—are then likely to be left increasingly to the developing countries which generally have a surplus of labour and whose economic growth will be increased, not necessarily by increases in productivity, but by drawing available labour more fully into production. This is the process by which a large part of the economic growth in European countries has been created and sustained in recent years.

There could be accompanying effects. As certain industries are left more to the developing countries, the latter's capacity to buy should be enhanced. They will consequently improve as markets for the developed countries—and increasingly as commercial markets, instead of as aid markets. Again, as the developed countries concentrate on particular industries, their need for wider markets will increase. They will still find their major markets within their own frontiers or within the frontiers of the developed world. But their need for marginal markets to absorb the full output of the industries with enhanced productivity should increase, just as the purchasing capacity of the developing countries enlarges through the growth of labour-intensive industries within their frontiers. Although the detail cannot become clear until the process is a good deal more advanced, one can see some prospect of an equilibrium emerging in this way and replacing or at least modifying in some measure the disequilibrium of the present time.

The process can have advantages not only for developing countries but also for countries which lie somewhere between the developing countries of Africa and Asia and the mature, industrial economies in the North Atlantic and Japan. Australia may be taken as an example. So long as the developed countries experience massive growth within their own economies, they do not need to look elsewhere for markets. Recent years have given plenty of evidence of this. In some recent periods, some of the EEC countries have achieved an increase in their exports to their partners in the EEC in a single year equal to the whole of their trade with the rest of the world outside the North Atlantic countries. In other words, they would have had to double their trade in a single year with the whole of the developing world (plus the Soviet-bloc countries, Japan, Australia and New Zealand) to win from that area export gains equal to those which they won from their EEC partners. The reality was that their trade with the developing world was relatively static and the greatest efforts could have achieved only a marginal result compared with the easy gains in trade with the North Atlantic countries. Therefore, the developed world has been overwhelmingly pre-occupied—despite aid targets and aid programmes and much conscience-ridden activity—with economic relationships among its own members.

However, if economic growth in the developed world slackens for reasons which we have hypothesised earlier and particularly if it declines to zero, serious changes could occur. These changes could be especially marked if there were a concurrent increase in the rate of economic growth in the developing countries, and in such countries as Australia and New Zealand, through the establishment of new industries or for other reasons; or if existing high rates of economic growth in some of these countries, such as Australia, are maintained. Then even small additions to export trade could take on a much greater importance than they do now. They could facilitate the maintenance of a more productive full employment of labour and capital and contribute to maintaining or increasing the rate of economic growth. This might be the result, especially if the developing countries were to provide markets for some of the production of the more sophisticated industries in which the developed countries were able to achieve the greatest gains in productivity.

In these circumstances, a return to a situation permitting genuine negotiation between the developed and the developing countries might become a somewhat closer prospect. For example, we have noted that, in recent years, Australia has not been able to negotiate effectively with European countries for improved access for agricultural products because European countries have not had such an incentive to obtain a share of the Australian market for industrial products that they have been willing to make concessions on agricultural access. However, if in the future, the rate of economic growth in Europe were to falter, the large market for industrial products in Australia would take on a new importance. Increased sales in Australia could contribute to maintaining and perhaps allowing for increases in the output of the more sophisticated, especially capital-goods industries. To win these increased sales, the European countries would then have a greater incentive to negotiate limits to protection of domestic agriculture or protection of particular products. They might also become even more interested in investment in Australia to finance these sales; but, in order to make this investment viable over the longer term, they would once again probably be required to take a much harder look at their policies of agricultural protection and to negotiate this protection downwards in response to Australian pressure. Much the same sort of thing, though varying in points of detail, would be likely to happen with the developing countries and with other countries which have not yet reached full industrial maturity.

All of the above is based on the assumption that the labour force in the developed economies is likely to remain static or nearly so in the future. It assumes that these economies will want to maintain much the same balance between remunerative work and leisure as there is today and that they will not want to draw into remunerative work labour which already exists within the economy but which is now unused.

If the economy and the society are prepared to accept a variable balance between remunerative work and leisure and if they are willing to draw presently unemployed or unremunerated labour into the economy, then what has been said about a situation with a static labour force will not apply. This more intensive use of labour will create a fundamentally new situation. It will not call for a permanent and unalterable change in the balance between work and leisure but it will involve periodic variations in this balance. In turn, this will require some changes in economic, managerial and social attitudes.

But it will do more than that. It will make the developed countries much more productive and it will also make them much more stable at a higher level. As against that, it will not necessarily increase the interdependence between the developed and the developing countries, in the way that the problems of a static labour force and the perhaps consequent more intensive international division of labour might do.

In any event, however, there would, as we have noted, be factors inhibiting against too quick and too complete a change in the

existing international division of labour, even in the context—
perhaps especially in the context—of the problems arising from
a static labour force. The more intensive use of labour might
both make more resources more easily available from the developed countries for the development of the poorer countries;
and it might also create such abundance and stability in the
advanced countries that it will be easier to move labour away
from the labour-intensive industries. There will still be some
inhibiting factors, including especially those which are essentially
social, political and strategic. But much of the flesh of the
economic—or so-called economic—inhibiting factors should be
cut away and leave a situation in which the developing countries
could more easily exploit their labour advantages to the benefit
of all.

XII
The Problem of Food

Among the many problems which confront the developing countries, one of the most acute is that of food and nutrition. And it's likely to become worse. The populations of the developed countries are, for the most part, not doing a great deal more than reproduce themselves. Their 1965 population of 1037 million had increased to 1090 million in 1970 and is expected to be about 1275 million in 1985. But that fairly gentle incline upwards does not apply to the developing countries. Their average annual population growth rate is about 2.6 per cent and going up. Their total population, which was 2252 million in 1965 and 2542 million in 1970, will have increased to 3658 million by 1985 and probably to something over 5000 million by the end of the century. Simply to maintain present nutritional standards, developing countries will therefore need twice as much food in thirty years' time as they consume now.

Will they themselves be able to produce it? It is far from certain that they will. The average annual economic growth rate of the developing countries was, according to the OECD, five per cent between 1950 and 1960, when the annual population growth rate was two per cent. Between 1960 and 1965, the annual growth rate was 5.1 per cent and the annual population increase 2.5 per cent. Between 1965 and 1969, annual growth rate went up to 5.8 per cent and annual population increase was 2.6 per cent. While the rate of population increase has therefore been going up about as quickly as the rate of economic growth, there has been a good margin in favour of economic growth.

But economic growth has not been confined to food production. Much of it has gone into industrial development; and, if developing countries are to be able to look beyond the single goal of nutrition or even if they are satisfactorily to reach that goal, they must industrialise. That is, in the end, the historical way out of the Malthusian nightmare. This does not mean that all development should be industrial development; but there should be balanced development in which agriculture and secondary and tertiary industry each will have an important place.

So far as food production is concerned, there have been, for the developing countries, both good signs and bad. In September 1970, the OECD's Development Assistance Committee found that, although malnutrition was the main factor limiting the development of human resources on which everything else depends, no progress had been made in solving the problem of malnutrition in 1969.

On the other hand, food production can, with good fortune, be increased sensationally. The newly discovered dwarf strains of wheat which have sparked off the 'Green Revolution', have enabled several developing countries to double their harvests in the last five years. In the past, India's annual wheat harvest averaged less than twelve and a half million tons; by 1969, the harvest had risen sensationally to more than twenty million tons. Much the same thing happened in Pakistan. Before the 'super-seeds' were used, Pakistan's wheat harvest was seldom more than four million tons; now it is more than eight million tons. These advances in production are tremendously important and postpone the ultimate crisis of population outrunning food supply. But the gains may be once-for-all gains. Newer, even more high-yielding crops may have to be developed at regular intervals if food supply is to keep pace indefinitely with population increasing at its present rate.

We should also be clear that the 'Green Revolution', at least at the present stage, does not offer the potential for a doubling of output of all food in all parts of the world. For the moment, it applies only to food grains and, for example, the new agricultural technology seems to operate best in irrigated areas. Therefore, we must reserve our judgement on whether and how far the 'Green Revolution' will solve the food production problems of all the developing countries and all food-producing regions within those countries. In any event, it is likely to provide a short-term rather than a lasting solution.

The needs of developing countries for food in the future will be massive. 'Need' is an incompletely economic term. The need for food may be defined as the amount necessary to enable people to ward off starvation or to work efficiently or to have a balanced diet or to have a standard of living equal to that of the high-income countries of the Western world. We may say that the need of the people of the developing countries is for one or other of these things. The present and prospective supply of food will be more or less adequate according to which of the definitions we adopt. There may now be less starvation, or in any event less mass starvation in the world than at any time in recorded history. Resources exist to meet a famine almost anywhere in the world and a will exists to move food quickly to meet such an emergency.

But, if fewer people actually starve, probably more people exist just above starvation level than at any earlier time. For populations have greatly increased. If wars, disease and starvation had continued to keep population down, those now surviving might live better with the resources available—although, of course, there is no guarantee that, in the different circumstances, the same volume of resources *would* be available. Since man has now won limited victories against his traditional enemies of war, disease and starvation, the greater number of survivors must cut the available cake into much smaller pieces.

If we are content to keep some hundreds of millions of people just above starvation level, then we can say that needs are just about being met already; and that this is not a situation which is unique in world history, except in terms of the size of the populations involved. On the contrary, it has been the norm. Only in recent years, in a relatively small part of the world have large communities, though a relatively small part of the world's population, lived confidently and continuously at a secure distance from the frontiers of starvation.

We may say too that, in achieving a breakthrough to, and even after the achievement of, higher and more secure standards of living, most of the people of most countries continued to live not very far above starvation level. Most people in the early years of the Industrial Revolution in England lived at such a level; indeed their standards were often below those of the agricultural and mercantile era which preceded it. The great conquests of North America and Australia brought little immediate comfort to those who carried out the conquest. The early years of the revolution in Soviet Russia similarly brought few material advantages to the mass of the people. In all of these situations, one, two or more 'lost generations' contributed heavily to the upward climb of mankind. The affluence of today was won with their sweat. They gave their skills and their energy, their courage and their endurance, all of which were vital to great economic advances, but they themselves—although they may have experienced other satisfactions—enjoyed few of the economic blessings which their children or their grandchildren derived from their sacrifice. If the lost generations had given less and taken more for themselves, the breakthrough to affluence for the generations which followed would certainly have been slower in coming and might never have been achieved at all.

So perhaps we may hypothesise that, in the developing countries, there must be some lost generations before affluence is to be achieved; it is perhaps an unavoidable purgatory on the way to riches. But a good deal of international thinking and international practice rejects or modifies such a spartan hypothesis. If the hypothesis is rejected, how can international arrangements be made which can put more food into the mouths of the world's hungry people without disrupting world production and trade?

First of all, we need to acknowledge that the magnitude of future food needs is massive, even on the assumption that nutritional standards remain static or improve only slowly. If income in India increases by only 2 per cent per capita per annum, an increase in population of less than 3 per cent a year—the actual increase is now about fifteen million a year—will require an extra twenty million tons of food-grains in 1975 and more than forty million in 1980. If we hypothesise that there will be *no* improvement in per capita income, India's need for food-grains will increase by about fifteen million tons in 1975—costing more than $1000 million even at prices for food-grains which we might regard as conservative—and more than thirty million tons in 1980—costing more than $2000 million or just about India's total current export earnings. The food problem in India is, of course, the most forbidding of any country in the free world, but the aggregate problem for all the poorer countries can be assessed in broad terms from the Indian situation and prospects. It provides us with some broad measure of needs against which to set prospective production and productivity.

In recent years, productivity has increased in all the countries with a highly developed agriculture. In North America, in Europe, in Australasia, much more food can be produced per acre and per man employed than twenty years ago, or even just a few years ago. For example, while acreage declined by about 10 per cent, average annual wheat production in Australia of about 146 million bushels in the 1940's increased to about 174 million bushels in the 1950's. Yield per acre went up from 12.8 bushels in the forties to 17.1 bushels in the fifties. By 1966-67, production had risen to about 467 million bushels from acreage about twice that in the fifties; yield had risen to 22.4 bushels per acre.

Acreage in the United States has been constantly restricted and constantly production has gone up. But as production has gone up, prices have tended to decline, especially in real terms, and the terms of trade have turned against the agricultural exporter. With some fluctuations, the tendency has been for the terms of trade of agricultural producers to stagnate or decline since the early 1950's. The incentive to maximise production and exports has declined because further production and exports are likely to depress prices still further and create more unsaleable surpluses.

The decline in the terms of trade has been caused firstly, by the inelastic demand for food in the richer countries and the ineffective demand in the poorer countries; and, secondly, by the diversion of demand in the poorer countries from agricultural to industrial goods. In the richer countries, as income increased, the volume of food consumption tended to level out and consumption shifted from the less expensive to the more expensive foods to give a more nutritious, more balanced and more attractive diet. This shift is not yet complete for the whole of the population in the developed countries but it has gone a long way. Some increase in aggregate consumption is still in prospect and, within this aggregate increase, some more pronounced increases in consumption are likely in such things as meat, dairy products and eggs. But these increases are likely to be much smaller than the potential or even the actual increases in supply. They are unlikely to provide an incentive for the full utilisation of resources currently available in the developed countries themselves.

On the other hand, needs in the poorer countries cannot express themselves in effective demand. A small part of the population lives at or above the average standard of living in the richer countries. The great bulk of the population lives considerably below this standard. Their income is devoted to the essentials of food, clothing and shelter but is sufficient to provide only a bare minimum, if that, of any of these needs. No upward definition of need will of itself provide the wherewithal for most people in the poor countries to acquire any more food than this bare minimum. A constantly increasing population will keep per capita standards forced down to this bare minimum level even though there may be rapidly increasing production. Increasing aggregate consumption will, therefore, be accompanied by an increasing aggregate unfulfilled need arising from contant levels of individual consumption multiplied by larger and larger numbers of needy individuals. These needs could be met if individual incomes were increased and that increase were directed to meeting food needs as a priority satisfaction. Alternatively, the price of food would need to be reduced while incomes remained constant.

There are some developing countries in which per capita income has increased or will increase substantially in the fairly near future. Mexico, Nigeria—despite the war—the Republic of Korea, Taiwan, Iran and a few other developing countries have already made good progress in economic development and might achieve further large improvements in per capita income fairly quickly and continuously. But in almost all countries there will be a constant struggle to keep the rate of increase in aggregate income ahead of the rate of increase in aggregate population.

This leads to the other element which has tended to turn the terms of trade against exporters of agricultural products. All developing countries need capital goods. Most of these capital goods cannot be produced domestically; they must be imported. Moreover, there is, rather paradoxically, an urgency about the acquisition of capital goods which does not apply in the same degree to the acquisition of consumer goods. Of course, if there is famine or an immediate threat of famine, then priority must be given to import of food. But so long as food consumption is maintained above the famine level or, in any event, at the level to which the population has been accustomed, then the urgency for acquisition of consumer goods declines. If this were not so— if developing countries felt a continuing urgency to import food up to the limit of their resources and so long as per capita consumption remained below that in the developed countries—then no resources at all would be available for the import of capital goods. Developing countries would, in effect, resign themselves to a continuing low level of income unless some fortuitous circumstances—a vast increase in external aid or the discovery of new natural resources—allowed some increase in living standards not dependent on domestic capital formation.

Developing countries are not willing to resign themselves to such a fate. Consequently, they seek to accumulate capital resources which, though they limit consumption now, will permit consumption to expand in future. Consumption is kept down to a minimum consistent, in per capita terms, with what the population has become accustomed to and consistent, in aggregate terms, with these per capita expectations and the increase in population. There may be some small variations around this minimum. Sometimes—because of increased population, poor prices for exports, a poor season with small harvests, unfulfilled expectations of external aid—consumption may fall below the minimum level. Sometimes—because of a sudden surge forward in export prices, especially good harvests, or an increase in external aid—consumption may increase temporarily above the minimum. But there will be a tendency for this minimum level which, in absolute terms, will vary among developing countries according to their past experience, to be the realised norm over a representative time-period. All the resources over and above this minimum, available to the developing countries, will in principle and, as far as possible in practice, be devoted to the acquisition of capital goods.

The developed countries which extend aid for the more rapid development of the developing countries, not only acquiesce in but strongly encourage this approach. This is natural and has a great deal of wisdom in it. However, it intensifies disequilibria already existing in international trade and international economic relations more generally.

The developing countries have limited export earnings and limited international reserves. They have much greater needs for capital goods for their economic development than their limited external resources enable them to buy. Ordinarily, those countries which do not produce enough food for their own requirements would have to use part of these external resources to buy food. Developed or richer countries with surplus food available therefore offer these countries aid in the form of food. The recipient countries are then able to meet their requirements for food—or a part of it—without making a call on their international resources, which they are then able to devote more fully to the purchase of capital or other goods for their economic development. The demand for these goods is already strong enough in a Keynesian system generally to absorb the total production of the developed economies within those economies themselves. This demand is intensified by purchases of the developing countries with a consequent effect on the prices of capital goods, on the terms of trade between agricultural and industrial exports, and on the dynamism of the suppliers of the capital goods, that is, the developed countries.

But the demand for food is not increased. Donor governments give food free, or on concessional terms, under various aid programmes, whether United States PL480 arrangements, Colombo Plan, World Food Programme or other arrangements. Generally, recipient governments sell this gift food on the normal market to middlemen or direct to consumers, at the same prices as if the free supplies of food had been bought on the world commercial market for scarce foreign exchange. There is no difference to the consumer. If he had to pay X for wheat bought commercially overseas, then he now has to pay X for wheat supplied to his government free. His effective demand is not increased. If his income is Y, then he can still buy only an amount of wheat equal to $\frac{Y}{X}$. His income has not been increased by the gift of wheat by another government. Therefore, his effective demand could be increased only by reducing the price to him of the gift wheat. If the price of wheat became $X - Z$, then he could buy, with constant income Y, $\frac{Y}{X - Z}$ and his effective demand—given the high elasticity of demand for food in the poorer countries—would increase. But this does not happen. Consumption remains the same. The only change is that scarce external resources are diverted from purchase of food to purchase of manufactured goods, mainly capital goods, needed in the development programme. In other words, the demand for the products of the highly industrialised countries is increased, while the demand for the products of the primary-exporting countries remains constant or, because of disposal of surpluses as gifts, is, in commercial terms, diminished.

There are some understandable reasons why the prices of food should not be reduced when food aid is received. For example, prices must be maintained for the domestic producer in the recipient countries. There are few, if any, cases in which all supplies of a particular type are imported. Some wheat will be produced locally and some imported; or imported wheat will be a substitute for local rice. If the price of imported supplies is reduced, it will depress the market for local supplies and probably depress the local economy more generally. Arrangements could be made, for example, through subsidies, to sustain the price to growers, even though market prices fall, but this would be more difficult in developing countries than in more sophisticated economies. Prices of food supplied as aid would need to be reduced in such a way that it would not disrupt or reduce incentives for increased agricultural production. Indeed, we must bear in mind that the maintenance of agricultural production will be vital to the developing economies. It will contribute to food supply and nutrition but, beyond that, it will provide employment and a demand base for industry until such time as the greater maturity of the economy and the emergence of an affluent consumer, comparable with the consumer now existing in the developed economies, provide sufficient employment in secondary and tertiary industries and sufficient demand for their products. In addition to all this, the maintenance and expansion of domestic agriculture will relieve the balance of payments of a burden of food purchases which—from such illustrative figures as we have quoted before—would almost certainly be beyond the export-earning capacity of most food-importing developing countries in the foreseeable future.

However, apart from the need to protect the domestic agricultural producer, there is another consideration. Food aid serves major purposes, subsidiary or supplementary to alleged provision of nutrition or actual provision of foreign exchange. When it is sold by the recipient government, the proceeds are used by the government to overcome shortages of budget revenue and to meet local costs of development projects. Domestic resources for economic development are scarce and their mobilisation is difficult, so that, even to meet only local costs of development projects might compel governments to embark on deficit financing, with consequent inflationary effects and loss of confidence in the currency. The sale of food provided as aid helps solve this problem. Food aid thus provides a solution simultaneously to the shortage both of external funds and budget revenue.

If food provided as aid were not sold but were distributed free to consumers, the recipient country would still achieve a foreign-exchange saving (although demand would increase and provide pressure for further imports), but any budgetary benefit would be lost. If the food is not distributed free, the benefit to the budget will depend on the price at which it is sold. In principle, therefore, some sort of balance might be struck between the objective of providing cheap food to consumers and obtaining the maximum benefit for the budget. This could be done by setting a price somewhere between free gift and the prevailing market price. In practice, food aid is generally sold at prevailing market prices. In reality, therefore, food aid is, for the most part, not food aid at all. It is a means of disposing of surpluses—which are not in practice disposed of in aggregate, by this means, any more than they would be by commercial sales—and of releasing foreign exchange and providing budget revenue to finance development. Food aid is a different form of capital development aid which could be given in the form of cash or the direct supply of capital goods. That it is given in the form of food does not change its nature. Although it is a most valuable form of aid, of great benefit to the recipient country, it does not raise the level of food consumption or nutrition in the recipient country. What it does is to permit minimum levels of consumption and nutrition to be maintained while the recipient country goes ahead with its capital formation.

To raise nutritional levels substantially during early and critical phases of capital formation would complicate the development process for many countries. Governments might find it desirable to keep rising expectations within limits which the economy can bear and which they themselves can control. So long as food consumption remains at low levels, there may be little unrest unless consumption falls still lower. But if levels are raised for any long period, then it may be necessary to maintain them at those levels if unrest is to be avoided. Therefore, even leaving aside the possible effects on local agriculture and budget revenue, governments might be unwilling to accept increased supplies of food aid which would raise consumption levels immediately but which would make governments more heavily dependent on continuing aid from overseas sources to maintain consumption at the newly accustomed levels.

Nevertheless, despite these problems, the raising of nutritional levels may be basic to the progress of developing economies on a broad front. This conclusion or at least hypothesis seemed to emerge from the meeting of the OECD's Development Assistance Committee in Tokyo in September 1970. The problem of malnutrition 'in varying degrees common to all developing countries, is the major factor limiting the development of human resources on which everything else depends. India provides the most obvious example of this problem. New solutions must be sought and applied quickly since increasing income offers no hope of a solution. It has been estimated that it would take thirty years, under the most favourable conditions, before the normal rate of increase of income, that is 3 per cent per year, would assure the minimum dietary requirements of only a third of the population. The Indian Government is aware of how urgent the problem is and seems ready to marshal its resources to find a speedy and effective solution to it.'[1]

However, even allowing for present complexities, the food problem now is nothing like as big and as complex as it is going to be. It is not a static problem. It is a magnitude which grows daily with the growth of populations. It may be that, huge though it now is and massively as it is growing in size, the developing countries will nevertheless be able to solve it themselves. The 'super-seeds' might provide the increased supply of food which is necessary, both because of their extra yield and because of the incentive which they provide for greater production by land-owners. This increased production might be enough to provide not only for the present population but also for the rapidly growing population of the next two or three decades. Dr Norman Borlaug, the American Director of the International Wheat and Maize Improvement Centre in Mexico City, who in effect launched the 'Green Revolution' through his development of dwarf strains of wheat, is reported to have said that 'we have only delayed the food crisis for another thirty years. If the world population continues to increase at the same rate, we will destroy the species.' A number of other experts—economists as well as scientists—agree with him.

It is not the increase in the population of the advanced countries which provides any serious threat to mass survival; it is the rapidly growing population of the developing countries which does it. Even with the benefit of the 'Green Revolution', it is likely that there will be many food crises before the end of the century and—unless there are further spectacular developments in pro-ducing food—there will be a crisis of wholly unprecedented dimensions about thirty years from now.

If there are any major disasters in the meantime, the massive crisis could be a lot less than thirty years away. If the new 'super-seeds', for example, were to be afflicted with disease difficult to cure or control—of the kind of potato blight in Ireland last century—mass starvation could quickly follow or threaten. A great deal of work is now going on and is projected, for example, within the Food and Agriculture Organisation assisted in some

[1] *Le Monde*, Weekly Selection, 23 September 1970, p. 5

measure by funds from the World Bank, in an attempt to avert these dangers. Resistant grain types are being preserved and new strains are being developed as an insurance against disaster. These are wise precautions, but they might not provide the complete insurance which their authors would like. If the insurance fails, millions might starve.

The threatened increase in population in the developing countries in the next thirty years is so great that people have thought mainly in terms of maintaining a minimum nutritional standard as population increases. That minimum would presumably be that operative in food-deficit developing countries such as India at the present time. If nutritional standards are to rise substantially—and if there is to be a margin against failure of the 'super-seeds'—food production will have to expand greatly beyond both present and prospective levels.

Unless nutritional standards are raised in the developing countries as part of a wider improvement in the level of living, it seems probable that present increases in population will persist well beyond the end of the century. (This assumes that no dramatic new means of limiting population growth within existing social structures will be discovered.) To achieve this improvement in living standards, rapid industrialisation and therefore rapid capital formation are essential. The movement upward in production and productivity and consequently in levels of living will then, hopefully, create social conditions which will banish the Malthusian spectre from developing countries.

It is possible that the worst may be averted. The population explosion could be less than we now expect—although the size of the population for the next few decades has been largely determined already. Even though we might hope for a problem less in magnitude, we should plan to meet a problem which is as great as our worst fears.

That means that we should both ensure that the developing countries achieve the maximum capital formation and industrialisation in the next few decades and that food production and food potential are expanded in both the developed and the developing countries. Expansion of food exports by the developed countries (such as the United States, Canada, Australia and New Zealand) can be useful principally in so far as they find outlets in the developing countries. Food markets in the developed countries are unlikely to expand sufficiently to take up substantially increased exports from other developed temperate primary producers.

Unless incomes are increased or the price of food to consumers is reduced, this increased quantity of food will not be marketable in the developing countries either. What might be necessary, therefore, might be some international subsidy arrangements which would ensure for producers in developed countries a remunerative price but which would make food available to *consumers* in poor countries *at a price which they can afford*. This would mean not merely the provision of food on grant or non-commercial terms by the rich to the poor countries. It would also require an incentive for the governments of the poor countries to make food available to their people at a price which would enable increased consumption and higher nutritional standards. Some plan may, therefore, be appropriate whereby the developed countries would make supplies of food available up to a declared level on a discount basis. For example, donor governments could supply food at sliding-scale rates. At a certain low level of imports, recipient governments would be required to pay full commercial prices. At a higher level of imports, the price which they were required to pay would be reduced for these imports. When imports reached a certain level which would have been fixed as a sort of quota beforehand in agreement among the developing and the developed countries, the price of all these imports would be reduced to zero, that is, food within the quota would be supplied free. This discount arrangement would be dependent on the recipient governments using the food supplied to increase food consumption, while maintaining domestic production. They would use supplies of food to reduce prices to the consumer and thus push up consumption. The quota, discount and price arrangements (including any necessary subsidies to domestic producers) would be such that the full quotas of food would be made available free by donor governments at the point at which consumption of food had been increased in the recipient countries to an extent agreed upon beforehand by donors and recipients.

Capital aid would have to be given simultaneously. Provision of food aid alone will not solve the underlying problem of population in relation to food supply; that can be done satisfactorily only by changing the economic and social structure. Therefore, governments will need to plan not only increased food aid and full development of the world's potential for food production, but also restriction of population growth and rapid development of secondary and tertiary industries.

Therefore, we need to plan for a substantial increase in non-food, non-agricultural aid if the problem of food and population itself is to be solved. The level of aid must be much higher than in the 1960's, when governmental aid was almost static in monetary terms at about $US6 billion and declined substantially in real terms. It probably should be at least doubled or trebled if a real start is to be made in tackling the threatening emergency arising from the population explosion.

This can be done only if there is a fundamental change in present Keynesian economic policies. It cannot be done unless arrangements can be devised to offset the damaging effect of large unrequited external outlays on the stability of the developed economies and unless, more generally, new means can be found for maintaining and restoring stability in the developed countries at the upper level of the economy. In other words, the basic solution to the problem of food in relation to increasing population in the developing countries is, like the solutions to other problems which we have described, production budgeting and stabilisation of the economy at the upper level through expansion of production. It will not solve the whole development problem immediately. The task will still be huge and complex. But no alleged solution will be effective without it.

XIII
Some Projections

There are two broad alternative ways in which the present situation may be projected into the future. The first assumes that present elements will continue to operate and that their effects will be carried to their logical conclusion. The second is that certain modifications will take place in the present situation and that there will be a substantial movement towards a new equilibrium.

What will be the result if present elements continue to operate unabated?

What will happen in the rest of the world will depend largely on what happens in the developed countries and especially in the North Atlantic Community. At the moment, it looks as though the members of the Community will continue to move closer together economically. There will be disruptions in this process. For example, in the European Economic Community, one would expect further movement towards integration although the resultant Community might be a good deal different from that originally contemplated under the Treaty of Rome. It might be an incomplete integration, perhaps in some ways closer to EFTA in its final than in its original conception; and it might operate in a context of political integration—if that proves to be the correct term—much less complete than many advocates within the European movement would wish. But the continuing pressures to form economic units larger than national economies—

especially bearing in mind the successes with which these efforts have already been attended—would seem sufficient to carry the Community forward to more rather than less economic integration in the future.

Much the same is likely to be true of EFTA. In much of its original conception, EFTA is greatly different from the European Economic Community. It aims at a free-trade area, not a customs union; it places less emphasis on elements of economic integration other than tariffs; and it is not—as so many proponents of the EEC see the Community—part of a total conception of political integration which it may stimulate and for which it may at the same time provide the first steps. But EFTA might find that it needs or will want to do some things which were not part of its original conception; and the EEC might find that it can do less than it has intended. At least in the immediate future, EEC and EFTA are unlikely to become identical. But both are likely to contain two essential features. The first is that they are likely to continue as areas of free trade or customs union in *industrial* products. The second is that each is likely to move towards greater co-ordination of economic policy—monetary, financial, budgetary, cyclical policy—though each Community might adopt its own individual procedures and techniques for realising this greater co-ordination.

The two most dramatic of Western Europe's economic Communities—the two with the most clear-cut personalities—might move therefore, in essential respects, in the same direction. There is nothing accidental in this. Nor is there anything in it which should be set down too simply as the peculiar achievement of statesmen within each of the two Communities. What is happening is a natural outcome of the recent economic situation and trends. For this reason, both communities have been remarkably successful in creating free trade areas in industrial products and show some promise of being successful more broadly in co-ordination of economic policies. In what they have achieved already, they have given further acknowledgement and impetus to existing trends. The present (1970-1971) negotiation by some EFTA countries, including Britain, to join EEC is a natural outcome of the similarities between the two groups and, more fundamentally, the similar economic situations and objectives of the individual member countries.

If this is so, it is likely that the conditions which have made the two communities successful will operate to push other industrial countries, at a similar level of development, along much the same route. This is what has happened and what, with luck, will continue to happen. While agricultural trade among the countries of the North Atlantic Community has (except in some ways within the EEC itself) become progressively more difficult, trade in industrial products has tended towards greater freedom. While GATT has been a failure as a regulator of agricultural trade, it has been a success in reducing tariffs and quantitative restrictions on industrial exports among the North Atlantic Community countries. GATT's success has not been the result of any intrinsic strength in its constitution or character but a reflection of the economic situation and trends which have moved the EEC and EFTA to a similar success.

The North Atlantic Community can therefore be envisioned as moving *towards* an industrial free trade area. It is far from being there yet. Tariff resistance, especially between the United States and Europe, is still high. The Kennedy Round negotiations contemplated a 50 per cent reduction in tariffs—mainly of the North Atlantic Community countries. Agriculture and exceptions reduced the extent of the across-the-board cut. Even if the aim of the negotiations had been originally confined solely to industrial products, it is perhaps unlikely that the full 50 per cent across-the-board cut could, in the best of circumstances, have been achieved; but a substantial cut was realised and a consequent substantial move was, as a result, made in the direction of a North Atlantic Community free trade area in industrial products. If this trend were continued and intensified, there would be a fair chance of achieving a free trade area in industrial products—or something approaching it—among all or most of the developed countries of the North Atlantic, with Japan ultimately perhaps being drawn in too.

However, a moment ago we mentioned parenthetically that a certain amount of good fortune might be necessary if this trend towards industrial free trade is to continue. The good fortune will turn on whether certain of the developed countries, especially the United States, adopt the 'right' economic policies at the right time. Although the United States enjoyed relatively high employment, a slide in the unemployment rate, and high economic growth conditions during the 1960's, inflationary and balance-of-payments strains caused serious policy problems and precipitated an induced recession in 1970. These difficulties have—in some ways paradoxically but nevertheless effectively—given strength to the movement for industrial protection in the United States, which never lies very far below the surface. As a result, it is conceivable that the Congress, and—more reluctantly—the Administration, might ultimately implement far-reaching industrial-tariff-protection policies and that there might then be retaliation against the United States by other developed countries. If this were to happen, it would fly in the face of recent economic trends and experience and would constitute an unnatural reversion to the Hawley-Smoot-type tragedies of the 1930's. Whether such tragedies can be averted is likely to depend, at least in some measure, on whether the United States Administration can find ways out of its present inflationary and balance-of-payments difficulties. Until the end of 1970, the Administration was fumbling its way without any clear direction or any real confidence that its policies would succeed. If it had persisted with past policies, it would have failed and Hawley-Smootitis might have got another obsolete spin. If the Administration's more recent change of policy towards reflation and expansion of demand and employment succeeds, the trend towards a widespread industrial free-trade area could be strongly resumed.

Not only this, but, if the right policies of stability are adopted, it is likely that co-ordination of economic policies will intensify. This form of policy co-ordination is already going on in EEC and, to a lesser extent, in EFTA; but also, in a less intensive but very real way, it has taken root in the Organisation for Economic Co-operation and Development, in which all of the North Atlantic Community countries plus Japan, are represented. Whether or not a North Atlantic free trade area is achieved, co-ordination of economic policies will be desirable and, we hope, will become increasingly regarded as essential if governments of developed countries are each to maintain high and stable rates of economic growth. But if and to the extent that further movement towards a free trade area is realised, the pressures for co-ordination of economic policies will be intensified. The experience within the EEC, as well as EFTA's experience of Britain's 'recovery' policies from 1964 onwards, has underlined how unrealistic it is to attempt to establish a free trade area or customs union without going a good deal beyond removal of internal tariffs and, in the case of a customs union, setting up a common external tariff; it is likely to survive only if the components of the free trade area or customs union apply economic policies which will allow the maintenance of a more general equilibrium among them. The recent—early 1971—Brandt-Pompidou understanding and the subsequent decision of the Council of the European Economic Community on economic and monetary union, though still vague and tentative—together with the possible enlargement of the Community—hold out a dramatic prospect for the future.

This prospect—it is a prospect, not a certainty—would have far-reaching implications for the rest of the world. If realised, it would mean that an industrial market unit, sustained by common economic and monetary policies, would be created which, if linked with North America, would dwarf anything known previously and which would reduce other areas of the world even more to the status of peripheral suppliers. An increasing proportion of world trade—already high—would be concentrated within the North Atlantic Community; and investment would be heavily concentrated there. This formidable economic entity stretching across the North Atlantic would dominate the world economy even more than the developed market economies do now; it would bestride the world economy like a colossus.

But this domination would not be wholly unqualified. The first and most obvious qualification is that the North Atlantic Community will continue to depend on other areas for some food and raw materials. A further considerable development of synthetics is probable and the Community could grow much more food than it does now. Even so, booming North Atlantic countries with a substantial growth rate will need a higher absolute volume of food and, more especially, raw materials in, say, 1980, than they do now. This demand is unlikely to put any more than temporary strain on the capacity of other areas to meet it, at least in the foreseeable future. On the contrary, recent experience is likely to be repeated and the expectation of increased demand in the North Atlantic Community countries is likely to call forth more supplies than are necessary to meet it. The way in which copper and nickel discoveries and production have responded to mounting demand is a recent illustration of the considerable potential which still exists to meet even what must be acknowledged to be the massive requirements of raw materials by the developed countries in the seventies and on ahead as far as we can see. There must come a time when the limits of the potential to produce new supplies of raw materials will be reached but it would be exercise in rash speculation to attempt to set down now when that moment might arrive. In the meantime, the North Atlantic countries' dependence on other areas for their supplies of raw materials is likely to be more than balanced by the demand of these other areas for manufactured, including capital, goods and by their needs for markets. While interdependence will not completely disappear, the imbalance in this interdependence is likely to increase.

A further qualification must be acknowledged to arise if there were a substantial slowing down of developed countries' growth rates. In some ways, this could provide the most effective means of reunification of the world economy. The highly industrialised countries could become more dependent on markets in the rest of the world. Some greater negotiating equality could be achieved. The question is how far this might be offset by technological advance in the highly industrialised countries, accompanied especially by more sophisticated and more perfectly co-ordinated policies of economic growth and stability. One can postulate as the extreme position that, if the highly industrialised countries can overcome the growth problem arising from a relatively static work force by improving and co-ordinating their economic policies, their independence—their introspection—and their domination of the world economy could become even more intense.

But there is another area in which the dependence of the rest of the world on the North Atlantic Community might increase. That is in food production. The food needs of the North Atlantic Community are likely to increase only slowly in future years— assuming a population growing only slowly in the next generation or so. The food needs of the rest of the world, on the other hand, are likely to grow alarmingly, because of huge increases in population, especially in Asia but also in Africa and other developing areas. Moreover, the growth and/or potential for growth in food production is likely to be in inverse proportion to the growth in population. What could happen therefore is that there will be constantly increasing surpluses or potential surpluses in the developed countries and constant or even constantly increasing food deficits in the developing countries; and that some new form of international arrangements might have to be devised to enable the surpluses to be applied to offset the deficits. If this happens, the degree of dependence of the rest of the world on the North Atlantic and other developed countries could increase still further. It could be a dependence extending to manufactures, capital and food.

One cannot foresee at present precisely how dependence for food supplies on the North Atlantic community might develop. The extent and nature of this dependence would turn on:

1 The rate of population growth in the developing countries;
2 Improvement in agricultural production in the developing countries;
3 The degree to which food production can be expanded in the North Atlantic community to meet needs in the rest of the world; and
4 The arrangements by which food surpluses from the North Atlantic community are made available to the rest of the world.

Meanwhile, and subject to continuing availability of sufficient raw materials, the prospect exists that the developed countries will grow more and more independent of the rest of the world. The developed countries are unlikely in the future any more than at present, to need to negotiate with the rest of the world and will have no stimulus to do so, unless their growth rates slow for avoidable reasons which we have already described. However, they will, for political and humanitarian reasons, wish to retain at least a minimum of political, economic and social stability in the rest of the world so that they can continue, undisturbed, with enlarging their own affluence. They will therefore make available to the rest of the world such resources as are needed or as they choose to make available to achieve this stability. The choice will be, essentially, for the developed countries to make. They will decide how much aid to give. They will decide the forms which aid should take. They will decide what trade advantages will be given to the developing countries, on what terms and for what period. If the experience of the past few years is repeated, the developing countries might not seem to be holding a begging-bowl to the industrialised countries; but unless there are major changes in the present situation, they will in fact have a bowl which will be filled or not according to the decisions of those countries which will, in the foreseeable future, dominate the world economy.

Perhaps that rather sombre picture is not entirely justified. There is an alternative—which we shall now look at briefly—to the extreme domination of the world economy by the industrialised countries. In any event, the picture just painted will not appear in such sharp chiaroscuro throughout the world. For example, some countries such as Japan and Australia already belong to or will shortly join the group of advanced, industrialised countries of the North Atlantic. But, geographically as in some other ways, they lie outside the 'community' of the North Atlantic countries. To some extent, they will inevitably be drawn into close relations with the community; but, to an important extent, they will continue to lie outside it. Relations with the developing countries, especially in Asia, will be much more important to such countries as Japan, Australia and New Zealand, than relations with the developing countries are to the North Atlantic countries. They will find an important part of their export outlets in the developing countries. They do now, or it is possible that they will invest, on a fairly large scale, in these countries. Because of the importance of these countries to them, they are more likely than the community countries to negotiate on a basis of equality with them.

These bridging operations between the developing countries and those who themselves provide a bridge to the traditional developed world are likely to be important to both parties. But they are unlikely to be sufficient to solve the problems of the developing countries. It may be too that, as the economies of such countries as Japan and Australia mature still further and as living standards (and wage costs) in Japan continue to rise, these countries will move more unequivocally into the group of indus-trialised countries of the North Atlantic community and become, in effect, members of that community, though geographically separate. It might be possible to arrest such a trend only if the industrialised countries so change their policies that all move together towards the creation of 'one economic world' which will restore the status of the developing countries.

This restoration of the developing countries' status can be achieved, *inter alia*, in the following ways:

1 By the developed countries moving out of the less sophisticated industries;
2 By the developing countries moving as speedily as possible into the industries vacated by their more advanced fellows;
3 By forced-draught development of the developing countries, involving:
   a Higher capital investment, especially in the less sophisticated industries;
   b Operation of joint projects in the developing countries by companies or governments of the developed and the develop-ing countries acting together;
   c Raising of consumption standards, especially of food.

One question which has to be asked is whether, if all these means were used to improve the economies of the developing countries, their negotiating position would be improved. The answer seems to be that, in the short and medium-term at least, it would not. The only way in which the bargaining position of the developing countries could be improved would be to establish (or restore?) the developing countries as markets and capital outlets of significance to the developed countries. In other words, there would need to be something of a return to the economic situation of the colonial era. At present, this seems highly unlikely. It is conceivable that there might be a return to a high degree of economic instability in the developed countries (arising, for example, from the adjustments necessary to cope with a relatively static working population). If so, the developing countries would almost certainly advance their status as markets and capital out-lets. But this prospect, although conceivable, is not a certainty nor even a probability. And, if it happened, it would raise other problems for the developing countries, even if it improved their negotiating position.

One of the questions involved in a better 'international division of labour' is whether the developed countries, by accepting such a division, would win any markets of significance in the developing countries. True, they would gain advantages. They should, by so doing, be able to raise their rate of growth or to contribute to its maintenance at a high level. And the developing countries, for their part, would be an important source of supply. Just as now, let us say, cocoa, must come from the developing countries, so, in the future, the only sources of supply for certain types of textiles might be in the developing countries. However, while they could become increasingly important as a supply source, this could be increasingly offset by the mounting importance of the developed countries as a supply source, not only for manufactures, but also for capital and perhaps even food. On the market side, it is doubtful that, in the foreseeable future, the significance of the developing countries as markets for the developed countries would change in any fundamental way. In fact, if and as the latter move over to more sophisticated industries, the significance of developing countries' markets might decline, because they would not absorb any significant proportion of the production of the more sophisticated industries.

At least, this seems to be the short-term result. In the longer-term, some movement towards greater equality in bargaining power might emerge. But in the short-term, the benefit of a better international division of labour is likely to be of a different kind. It is likely to move developing countries away from arbitrary aid towards a still somewhat arbitrary but more satisfying and perhaps more stable dependence on trade—on earned income. This would give the developing countries some of the same advantages which they might gain from successful negotiation.

For example, two of Australia's main exports have traditionally been wool and wheat. Access to many European markets for wheat has been dependent on negotiation—on Australia being able and willing to grant import concessions to European countries sufficient to induce those countries to ease access for Australian wheat. But wool has usually been on a different basis.

Access to European markets has usually been free—and probably will continue to be whether there is any negotiation or not. In other words, the strength of the marketing position for wool depends on the demand for the commodity itself and the fact that it is not produced in quantity in many of the main using countries. To this extent, its position is much stronger than wheat or other commodities which may hold or extend their market position only in so far as Australia can give something in return which the developed market economies really want.

Much the same applies to the developing countries. Cocoa is not produced in the main markets in the North Atlantic community. Therefore, cocoa will find a market there no matter how weak the negotiating position of the tropical developing countries. The question is how far the range of such commodities— secondary as well as primary—can be extended. The expansion of trade in this way would, as Professor Gottfried Haberler has pointed out, assist growth through, *inter alia*, the provision of essential imports and the probable stimulation of an increased inflow of technology and capital.

Much depends on the will of the developed countries to agree to such an extension or expansion. But their real self-interest— though not clearly negotiable—could be involved in it. Much will turn on the rate of economic growth which will be possible in the developed countries without the latter changing their relationships in any fundamental way with the developing world. If growth rates of 4 to 6 per cent or above can be readily maintained without any such fundamental changes, then the incentives to make structural economic changes will not be related to growth, although they may still be persuasive. Many of these incentives will be wholly or almost wholly non-economic.

If growth rates were to slacken in the developed countries, they might tend to look round for ways of restoring them. They might search with especial care if the slackening of growth rates tended to be permanent. What this might mean is that a fundamental change in the economic relationships between the developing and the developed world might depend on a further accentuation of the disequilibrium in the rates of population growth in the two areas. If the working population of the developed countries tends to stagnation or declines, there could be growing pressure to achieve a new international division of labour which would give the developing countries a more dynamic role in the world economy. However, there must be grave uncertainties whether the logic of this situation would be pursued. It seems much more probable that, faced with a difficult domestic economic situation, in which growth in national product has been seriously reduced, the governments of developed countries would seek their salvation in the illogic of increased tariff protection for declining industries rather than in concentration on those industries which showed the richest promise of growth.

That brings us, finally, to the theory that the developed countries, by a more intensive use of labour already within their economies, might achieve a better equilibrium both within their individual domestic economies and the developed world as a whole and also a better equilibrium between the developed and the developing countries. For the latter, it would still be an equilibrium of dependence but it would be a dependence which the developed countries should be better able to sustain and not one which would go directly and acutely against their own economic interests and disrupt their own economic stability. In an imperfect world, it would be an imperfect solution; but it might provide an equilibrium for the sustained period necessary for an equilibrium more solidly based on mutual interdependence to emerge.

Let us pursue this just a little further.

A Working Party of the Economic Policy Committee of the Organisation for Economic Co-operation and Development recently published a report[1] which seems to deliver the *coup de grace* to policies of demand control. 'The experience of the 1960's,' the report said, 'shows that, at the kind of demand pressures which have obtained in the past decade, a substantial long-term upward pressure on prices persists. It is evident that if demand management policies could achieve a smoother pattern of growth, the exceptional pressure on prices which develops in the later stages of booms could be reduced. But no country has found it possible to eliminate pressure on prices simply by holding down the pressure of demand. When margins of excess capacity have emerged which might have been large enough to induce much

[1] *The Growth of Output 1960-1980*, December 1970

more stability in the process of income/cost determination, governments have invariably judged that the objectives of high employment and growth required the re-expansion of demand. Furthermore in the short term, demand management can have a perverse effect on prices, as productivity growth tends to drop at the start of a slowdown.'

Elsewhere, the report maintains—with a great deal of validity —that incomes policies have encountered difficulties, and thrusts the solution to the problem of price stability on to the politician rather than the economist: 'the problem of price stability is ultimately a political rather than a technical one—the problem of extending government responsibility and action into new areas'. But the report itself enlarges the dimensions of the problem for, in its introduction, it says that 'economists have always been aware that human welfare is not identical with marketable output. But this remained largely a theoretical qualification as long as marketable output of the necessities of life was in short supply. But with contemporary technologies and living standards, it is doubtful how far the growth of marketable output, as defined in national income statistics, is an adequate measure of the growth that is important for society.' So the market mechanism cannot adequately resolve priorities between the competing needs of the society: 'for a growing part of the needs are no more of an individual character; the importance of goods and services such as education, health or the amenities of city life are not susceptible of any ordinary market valuation; and the length of the time horizon and the size and complexity of the questions involved may exceed the capacity of market mechanisms to supply rational answers'.

While there are few who would argue with this, the need of advanced societies for satisfactions which lie outside marketable output will undoubtedly intensify—probably greatly intensify— the problem of demand management. It is likely to reveal even more conclusively the inadequacy of demand management in the modern situation. Stability and growth—domestic equilibrium— as well as external equilibrium encompassing, *inter alia*, the relationships between developed and developing countries are likely to be revealed as needing something much more than— something much different from—demand management or demand management alone. It is likely to require production control and production budgeting with the emphasis on stabilising the relationship between production and demand by moving up production at the upper level of employment of the advanced economy. That is the projection of the present situation or the variation of the present situation to which we must look.

XIV
Conclusion

There is some tendency to think sometimes that the major characteristics of the industrial era have been constant—constant over
two hundred years since the beginning of the Industrial Revolution in Britain and Western Europe. That, obviously, is not so.
There is a similar understandable tendency to think that what is
now will persist; and, given the slow grasp of social realities by
the human mind, what is thought to be the situation now has
already passed, has already ceased to be.

The Industrial Revolution grew out of the society of its time
and that society was, in some important ways, only slowly
changed by it. The techniques altered, the methods of production
and exchange, the means of winning a livelihood. Cities grew,
populations increased; but the distribution of income and wealth
in the society remained unequal, indeed for a time it may have
become more unequal than before. Since production increased
but the incomes of most people did not, new markets had to be
found to absorb the new product if the new techniques and the
capital within which they were incorporated were to be fully
employed. An increase in domestic population provided some
part of the new market; the opening up of foreign markets provided other outlets. These new markets provided also many of
the supplies for the new industry and a destination for some of the
capital accumulated from the profits of new production and new
economic organisation. A situation in which the consumer any-

where was not much different from the consumer everywhere provided an incentive for the extensive penetration of markets and for the incorporation of the whole world into the marketing area of the industrialising economies.

This situation also provided a basis for the further development of the industrial economy. The employee-producer, by consuming less than his product, provided a margin to the employer-producer whereby the latter could accumulate capital for the further sophistication of his industrial processes. But, for this to happen, the margin of production not absorbed by the employee-producer had to be sold through the extensive cultivation of external markets, otherwise the sophistication of industrial processes would lose any purpose and the process would be brought to a halt.

Cyclically, this did, in any event, occur.

And because it occurred—and occurred, perhaps not so much with greater frequency as with greater intensity—the system had to change or adapt, otherwise it would have been replaced by revolutionary means. Of course, the process of production was never brought entirely to a halt. But sometimes it seemed that it would be. The prolonged, world-wide Great Depression of the 1930's seemed sometimes to threaten the whole fabric of the economy, the society, and the political systems of the time, and the unemployment was so massive that economies sometimes seemed to be at or near a standstill.

And so a major adaptation had to be made. It was made. The economy seemed, by this adaptation, to be preserved in much the same form as before. Or, more than this, it seemed to be preserved in much the same form but with the cyclical disasters, the chronic less-than-full employment and its sinful imperialism put to flight. The adaptation represented by the Keynesian system after the Second World War did, indeed, carry these benefits with it. In many respects, it was all that those who had endured the terrible 1930's could have dreamed of. But it had characteristics whose implications were only slowly perceived.

Apart from relative economic stability, it brought affluence. Everyone was rich. Perhaps that needed some qualification; the old and the invalid and the unemployed, the deserted wives and the unemployables were far from rich but the situation of even these exposed groups was greatly improved within the general affluence. Those who worked and had ability could become richer than any emperor of any earlier time. There are said to be 200,000 millionaires in the United States alone and there are thousands in the rest of the developed world. But, quite apart from the millionaires, the mass of the population of the developed countries have a command over economic resources undreamed of before. And this command over economic resources—this affluence—together with its stability or, better still, its dynamic growth has changed the perspective of the modern, developed economies.

They look inwards, not outwards. They feed on themselves and nourish themselves; they no longer feed on or nourish colonies or other developing countries in a different economic league from themselves. But no group of developed countries can really live like that—in preoccupied isolation. They need supplies and they have political, strategic and humanitarian reasons for continuing relationships with the developing world. In the attempt to face and deal with this reality, they—or some of them—give economic and technical aid, provide private capital and extend defence support and aid and protection. In so doing, they risk encountering economic difficulties themselves. If their expenditures go too far—even though their gross national product may be increasing rapidly and much more than their overseas expenditures—their own equilibrium will be upset. When they try to restore their own equilibrium, they do so by trying to revert to another earlier disequilibrium of deflation. But, in practice, they can't do this any longer. The affluent society created by the Keynesian system won't allow it. The attempt, in which all developed countries' governments still persist, makes the situation worse: it makes more acute both the disequilibrium within the developed economy and the disequilibrium between the developed and the developing economies. Unemployment grows; inflation grows; the balance of payments deficit persists; and aid to developing countries, in real and perhaps in monetary terms, declines.

And so a time has again come, about a quarter of a century after the widespread implementation of Keynesian policies, for another major adaptation to be made in our system.

The essence of the Keynesian adaptation was that demand should be maintained, where necessary by government and central-bank intervention, at a level sufficient to ensure full employment. The new adaptation would not interfere with that. What the new adaptation would do is, in essence, to ensure that stability is maintained, at the upper level of the economy, not by an almost inherently ineffectual attempt at suppression of demand but by a stimulus to production which will move supply to an equilibrium with demand at or above the level of use of resources which is now regarded as full employment.

This is the adaptation of an economic system which we must now make. This is the essence of the theory of general equilibrium in a Keynesian system which we have adumbrated in what has gone before. Let us now set down that theory in summary form, together with some economic policy implications which go with it.

First of all, let us postulate that the centrepiece of modern economic policy is the achievement and maintenance of full employment. That means that labour and capital—but especially labour—should be employed as fully as possible as much of the time as possible. There are—once the thing gets properly under way—no ifs or buts about this. It is not just fairly full employment now and again. It is all employed always. Anything less than that constitutes a political, social and economic illness.

There are qualifications, of course, because there have to be qualifications. New labour—adolescent or immigrant, for example —comes on to the market and instant employment is not always feasible. A postman in Boomville decides that he wants to be a gardener in faraway Roseville and it takes him a while to get settled into his new job.

But the qualifications have to be as few as possible and as small as possible. And they have had to get fewer and smaller as time has passed. Twenty-five years ago, an unemployment rate of 4 per cent looked good; and so it was, compared with an unemployment rate often much worse than 10 per cent during the 1930's. But 4 per cent came to look like a disaster rate in most countries in the 1950's and 1960's. Some countries began to think in terms of 2 per cent or even 1 per cent as the norm. This was the rate which should be maintained most of the time—if, indeed, it could not be maintained all of the time. If the norm is 2 per cent, then a slide in unemployment to 3 per cent is a bad slide. Half as many people again are unemployed over and above the number which has come to be acceptable to the community. If the norm is 1 per cent, a slide of only a half per cent to an unemployment rate of 1½ per cent looks like a near-disaster to a community accustomed to having virtually everyone working virtually all the time.

So margins get narrower. The acceptable rate of unemployment tends constantly to be reduced and the acceptable deviation from that rate tends constantly to be reduced also.

This partly explains why the operators of a Keynesian economy fail to maintain stability of that economy especially at the upper level of the economy. In theory, all that is necessary to turn the economy downwards is to reverse the process which turned it upwards. But this theory would work in practice only if a government were prepared to call into operation much the same economic imperatives as those which operated before the Keynesian era. Wages and prices would be stabilised if the economy were to be subjected to the staggering blows of the 1930's. But that's out of the question. A government will talk of taking the steam out of the economy and it will adopt fiscal and monetary measures to get the steam out. But not much steam. Just a little. And the more often it acts to take that steam out, the less steam it is in fact able to take out. It acts less and less to do less and less all the time.

And nobody must suffer. Not materially anyway. Inevitably most people will suffer some spiritual hurt if the economy rejects them at all, for however short a period. But, if governments are still prepared to inflict this hurt on an ever decreasing number, they are progressively more insistent that the spiritual hurt be accompanied by the smallest possible material hurt. Social service benefits must be high. Unemployment benefits must be high. Perhaps not quite as high as if the breadwinner were still working but—especially taking account of continuing family benefits—not much lower.

So this reduces the margins still further. Consumption levels remain high. So high that it would take a massive assault on employment levels to effect any substantial downturn in the economy. And this, as we have just seen, is politically unacceptable.

So when a government seeks to take the steam out of an overheated economy, it is seeking to do what is impracticable by its own standards—and from what is now its own long experience. The government just can't do it.

But it continues to make the attempt. And this attempt has very important consequences. They are not the consequences which the government seeks. And often they are consequences which are partly unrecognised. But that does not make them any less significant.

The effort to deflate the economy takes some labour—not too much, but some—labour off production and reduces the output of some labour which remains in production but which works shorter hours through reduction or elimination of overtime. Most fiscal and monetary measures hit one industry—such as the building industry or the automobile industry—harder than others, so that there has to be movement of labour from one industry to another. This movement might be fairly quick and might not show up in unemployment statistics or not show up for long; but it cuts down gross production.

But, in the meantime, consumption remains high. It will probably fall somewhat under the impact of fiscal and monetary measures which were intended to achieve that objective. But it can't fall far for reasons we have already explained: unemployment cannot be allowed to rise too high; and those who are unemployed must, as far as possible, be spared from any material suffering. Savings accumulated in the good period are used by workers or those unemployed to maintain consumption in the less good period. The result is that production may fall more than consumption. This will have a number of effects.

The first is that less demand will be chasing relatively even less supply. Prices, instead of going down—as the government would have wanted in trying to cool down the economy—will tend to go up.

The second is that trade unions, seeing some of the gilt taken from the gingerbread of the boom, will seek to find compensation in increased wages. The continuing surge forward in prices will provide both an incentive and a justification for these intensified demands. The result will be—once again contrary to the objectives of the government—a surge forward in wages; and again this will react on prices.

The third is that the government's deflationary measures, since their immediate impact will almost certainly be concentrated on selected industries, will divert demand from those industries to other industries. For example, the government might have considered that the boom had a large part of its origin in excessive activity in the building industry and might therefore have applied restrictions to that industry through, for example, housing finance. The result might be—probably with some time-lag—not only an inflation of house-rents but also increased demand for other consumer durables with probable rises in their prices.

The fourth is that additional expenditure will be directed to imports to the extent that domestic production falls relatively more than consumption, and to the extent that expenditure on imports can be substituted for expenditure on domestic goods and services. There is a danger that a government's attempt to deflate might divert expenditure from, for example, the building industry, that is, from domestic goods and services, to, for example, consumer durables and luxury goods imported from abroad. The result might be a deterioration in the balance of payments which, in turn, might stimulate the government to take further deflationary measures in an attempt to recover the external position. A spiralling trend towards apparently chronic disequilibrium might result, with pressures developing for 'fundamental' adjustments such as variation in the exchange rate.

The fifth is that there will be a loss of confidence in the short-term, and perhaps also in the longer-term strength of the economy. Domestic investment is likely to be reduced. Stock markets are likely to be depressed. The inflow of capital from abroad is likely to be halted or reduced. Residents with funds available for investment are likely to take more interest in investment opportunities abroad and less interest in investment opportunities at home. If the government takes no special defensive measures, the result will be an immediate deterioration in the balance of payments through the capital-movements sector and a prospective reduction in the productive capacity of the economy to meet future domestic and export demand, because of the cut-back in domestic investment.

The sixth is that there will be a tendency for labour to move out of the economy and for movement of labour into the economy to be deterred. In other words, net immigration will be reduced or net emigration will be increased. The result will be a further reduction in production, a further disincentive to investment, and further disequilibria, first, between domestic supply and demand and, second, in external trade and payments.

What this amounts to is to say that to attempt to reverse the Keynesian mechanism to bring an economy off the boil is not merely ineffective but positively damaging. It constitutes—if it were really implemented—an attempt to turn the clock back. It would be an attempt to apply 'remedies' which were involuntarily applied in an earlier economic era—most dramatically in the 1930's—but which have been categorically rejected by an ever-increasing range of countries since 1945. To reverse the Keynesian mechanism now results only in intensified domestic and external equilibrium. As a means of achieving economic stability, it must therefore be rejected. An alternative mechanism must be found.

This alternative mechanism must be found not only for reasons of stability of individual national economies—that is, individual national economies of the *developed* countries—which are the only countries for which Keynesian policies are really relevant. An alternative mechanism must be found for reasons also of mutually beneficial relations between the developed and the developing countries and in order to carry through, as quickly and efficiently as can be managed, the economic development of the developing countries.

At the moment, what happens is this. All the developed countries have moved to conditions of full employment, at which point ideally there is an equilibrium between internal demand and supply and external payments. The introduction of any additional element of demand or failure of supply will upset the domestic balance; and, as part of this, the introduction of any unusual element in external outlays will upset the external balance. Minor and temporary dislocations can be borne. For example, an industrial strike will disrupt production and supply but, although it might be temporarily painful, it is unlikely to cause a major upset to the economy unless it is particularly widespread and lasting or it is superimposed on other elements tending to create disequilibria. Again, limited commercial credits, economic aid and capital movements can be sustained, especially if there is a flow-back of earnings which reduces net outflow in any one year. But a persistent and substantial outflow of capital, economic aid, defence and defence support expenditure overseas and expenditure related to colonial responsibilities and other non-economic activities are unlikely to be sustained without creating serious disequilibria.

The balance is normally fairly fine. If a country, for reasons of history or tradition or because of its responsibility as a great power, is involved in extraordinary external outlays of a large and sustained kind, this balance is likely to be upset. If a country, accustomed to a large capital outflow because of its experience in an earlier economic era, seeks to sustain this outflow, its external payments balance may be disturbed. Similarly, if a colonial power continues to shoulder major colonial burdens, these outlays will, in themselves, tend to disrupt the external payments balance so long as the colonial power seeks to implement Keynesian policies in its domestic economy. If a great power undertakes expenditure on large defence establishments at home (perhaps including space expenditures) and overseas, extends defence and economic aid and permits a major outflow of private capital, it will, after a time, be confronted with balance of payments difficulties which will compel a major revision of its political and economic policies.

There may be a temporary escape from this dilemma. If substantial foreign reserves have been built up in an earlier period or if a currency is cushioned through its status as a reserve currency or if there is a substantial inflow of capital or if certain phenomena such as the discovery and export of massive quantities of minerals give an extraordinary boost to overseas earnings, a long period of unusual outlays may be possible. But the end is inevitable. Sooner or later, in a Keynesian system, extraordinary outlays must be balanced by extraordinary inflows or, at least, the margin of imbalance must be fairly small and discontinuous.

To achieve and maintain economic stability, therefore, the safest course is to concentrate on development of the domestic economy. The old policies of extensive capitalism—often carrying with it some or other form of colonialism—are dead or dying or disadvantageous. They have been replaced by policies of intensive capitalism. The developed economies, from being extroverted, have become highly introspective, preoccupied with their own development, their own employment, their own gross national product.

Like almost anything, this allegation of introspection can be exaggerated. The developed countries have not abandoned international trade. Far from it. Their foreign trade—individually or collectively—is greater than ever before. The developed countries have vastly expanded trade among themselves; but they have also increased their trade—absolutely, though not relatively—with developing countries. Generally the developing countries are selling more primary products to the developed countries than ever before; and the developed countries need these supplies as food for their people or raw materials for their industries.

The introspection of the developed countries is not measured in these terms. But it is real nevertheless. Firstly, although virtually *all* international trade has increased since 1945, trade among the highly developed countries has increased vastly more than any other sector of international trade. The most dynamic and relatively stable markets for the developed countries are their own domestic markets and those of other developed countries. The least dynamic and least dependable and stable markets are those of the developing countries.

Secondly, the developed countries look for capital exchanges with their fellow developed countries. They look for an inflow of capital from these countries and they look for investment opportunities in those same developed countries. Most of them will experience a two-way flow of capital; some of them will be net exporters of capital to other developed countries, others will be net importers of capital from other developed countries. This does not mean that they will not have some investment interest in the developing countries. Indeed, all of them do. But their interest will be small compared with their interest in investment in their own domestic economies and in the economies of other developed countries. And the flow of investment in relation to developing countries will be almost entirely one-way: all of the developed countries, in so far as they invest in developing countries, will be net exporters of capital to the developing countries. This will mean that capital which could have been used at home will not be balanced by any compensating inflow, will be lost to the national economy and will have to be compensated for by some other element if balance is to be maintained in the balance of payments.

None of the above means that export trade with and investment in developing countries will have *no* value for the developed countries and particularly for individuals and companies within those countries. But it does mean that their importance to the national economy of each developed country will tend to be peripheral and, in the case of investment, the unrequited outflow of funds is potentially damaging to the developed economy. If a situation of disequilibrium emerges in the developed economy which compels or is believed to compel the government to embark on deflationary policies, then the unrequited outflow of funds to the developing countries might become extremely burdensome and perhaps intolerable. In these circumstances, the interests of the developed and the developing countries come sharply into conflict.

Fortunately or otherwise, depending on where you sit, conventional wisdom is such that this has not yet made any full or indeed noticeable impact on public consciousness. People still think along the lines that trade with and investment in the developing countries are advantageous to both parties. People think, for example, that trade with developing countries should be vigorously promoted even while they themselves are putting virtually the whole of their effort into the much more profitable venture of selling as much as they can on their own or other developed markets. 'I'm not doing it but I'm sure someone else should be' is the burden of their behaviour, if not of their declarations. Much the same is true of investment in developing countries, with the addition of a highly moral belief that investment should be at a high level to help the poor and the starving along the road first to sufficiency and then to affluence.

But even conventional wisdom eventually catches up with the facts. It is doing so now. The penny is beginning to drop that trade with developing countries just isn't of vital importance any more, generally speaking isn't worth negotiating for and might even, in circumstances of political and economic instability, be disadvantageous. Investment in these countries similarly is or gradually wiil be seen, firstly as a burden and secondly as a potential disaster.

When this realisation is complete, not only will the world be divided—as it is now—into two groups of the powerful and the peripheral, but the justification for the division will, at that point, be seen to be compelling. It is the political pressures for aid and trade, rather than economic advantage for the developed countries, which give the developing countries a greater part in international exchanges than they would otherwise have. When the public realisation dawns that the political and charitable impulses to aid and trade are even more dominating—and damaging—than had been supposed, the public willingness to support these burdens at the cost of acknowledged sacrifice of economic benefits is likely to decline sharply. The rich countries will become more introverted; the poor more neglected.

Is there any way in which this denouement might be avoided?

There is a solution as simple as the original Keynesian adaptation to our economic system. The Keynesian adaptation dealt with the problems of the economy essentially at the lower level of employment. The new adaptation would deal with the problems of the economy caused but not solved by the Keynesian adaptation, that is, the new adaptation would deal with the problems of the economy at the upper level of employment.

The Keynesian adaptation was concerned essentially to stimulate demand; and the economic policies which flowed from it were, therefore, aimed at stimulating or suppressing demand, and it was from this that changes in employment and production flowed. While the Keynesian adaptation and the economic policies which flowed from it were, in theory, concerned with the level of demand at both the lower and the upper level of employment of the economy, they were, in practice, much more concerned with stimulating demand at the lower level of the economy to get it out of a depression. The new adaptation, while it acknowledges that stimulation of demand is an appropriate solution to problems at the lower level of employment of the economy, postulates that stimulation of production is the appropriate solution to the problems at the upper level of employment of the economy.

Although production must be the primary preoccupation at the upper level of the economy, if stability is to be maintained, demand must nevertheless be a simultaneous, though secondary, preoccupation. Demand must be held down while production is pushed up, so that an equilibrium between demand and supply is achieved at a level at or above what we now regard as the level of full employment of the economy.

If this new adaptation is implemented, it will achieve three major purposes—and three major benefits will flow from it. It will move up the level of production, thus increasing the gross national product and the level of per capita income; it will stabilise the economy at the upper level, this upper level being, after the adaptation, that which we now regard as full employment, or above; and it will provide at least a partial solution to the problems of the economic relations between the developed and the developing countries and, in particular, allow a greater flow of capital and aid, on a more stable basis, from the former to the latter.

The first major benefit is an increase in production. Is it in fact feasible to increase production at the upper level of the economy? Can the theory on which the adaptation is based be related to the practical realities of the economy?

The answer to both these questions is 'yes'. Production can be increased and the adaptation applied most simply by using more intensively labour resources already within the economy. Part of these labour resources are now used but not used completely; the other part is not used in the market economy at all.

Therefore, production can be increased by using more completely labour resources already engaged in production and/or by drawing into production labour resources which are now not used at all. To put this in more explicit terms, carpenters and factory workers and dairy farmers and timbergetters can work longer hours for more money or take a second (part-time or full-time) job. Older persons can be drawn into production over the whole range of the skills which they have acquired in their working lives; and so can married women. In all cases, training programmes can be instituted to extend the range of skills of the individual and to bring out his potential for production. In a free economy, additional labour will, of course, have to be freely offered in response to incentives. Similarly, employers will engage additional labour in response to the incentives of the market and special incentives provided by fiscal and monetary measures.

The amount of unused labour in the economy is enormous. In the emergency of a war, for example, in which it might be desirable to bring together the full productive resources of the country, the labour force could be increased by at least 50 per cent and probably more. This 50 per cent increase may not be possible over the whole range of labour—for example, it would probably not extend to the topmost management and professional skills—but it would extend over a very considerable range, sufficient to move the economy up to new and much higher levels of production in every major sector of the economy.

Not only is it possible to increase production beyond the present level for full employment and not only is the surplus of unused labour in the economy very substantial, but social attitudes in the modern, developed economy are such that comparatively little organisation and few incentives are needed to mobilise this labour for production. To put this more explicitly and simply, many more older people and married women would be willing to work for wages and salaries—and many more workers would be willing to work longer and take a second job—if it were made easy for them to do so and they got more money—enough more money—for it. Some groups—perhaps especially the older people —would welcome the chance to be productive or productive again in the economy.

Use of this labour would increase production much more than the value of the labour itself. It would permit the more intensive use of capital, particularly to the extent that capital installations could be used at full capacity for a longer part of the working week. The more intensive use of labour should, therefore, mean a less than proportionate increase in capital; additional investment expenditure should consequently be low relative both to additional production and to wage payments.

That brings us to the second major benefit which will accrue from an increase in production: restoration of equilibrium at the upper level of employment of the economy. An increase in production will increase wage payments and so add to demand. Tax incentives provided to bring forth that increased production will mean that a greater proportion of additional wages will be available as take-home pay, and so the impact of the additional wages on demand will be greater than normal.

However, there will be offsetting factors. Production will rise much more than the value of wages. The demand for capital should be relatively smaller than normal for the size of the increase in production. Much of the increase in wages and profits will be drawn off in taxation—despite the concessions—and should be neutralised.

The use of fiscal measures in this dual way, both to stimulate production and to hold back existing and new demand, will be vital to the success of the policy of stabilisation through increased production. Increased taxation revenues, together with a substantial reduction of some social service payments (especially unemployment benefits), should mean a substantial budget surplus, amounting to 10 per cent or more of the total revenue. But these calculations can be only in the most general terms. The exact impact of additional production on demand and the extent to which fiscal measures will be necessary to draw off this demand will depend on the particular circumstances of the economy at the particular time.

But the important thing is that it will be possible to keep additions to demand below additions to production. The first round of additions to production and to demand will set in train a multiplier effect, increasing production and demand up to perhaps three or four or five times the original additions. Fiscal and monetary measures will need to be sufficient again to ensure that the secondary production remains significantly above the secondary demand. Production must be stimulated; and potential accretions to demand must be simultaneously neutralised by fiscal and monetary measures to the extent necessary to allow production to move up to the level of demand.

What should happen in this process is that demand and supply should be brought into equilibrium at a level above that of either demand or supply when the process was begun. If at the beginning of the process, demand equalled X and supply equalled $X - Y$, at the end of the process demand will have moved up to X plus Z and supply will have moved up to $(X - Y)$ plus $(Y$ plus $Z)$ or X plus Z and the economy will be in equilibrium, without either inflationary or deflationary pressures, at a higher level of activity than before. In practice, the process is, of course, unlikely to work out with that degree of perfection and there will be miscalculations of the same kind as those which have occurred with Keynesian policies. But these miscalculations can be put right with less difficulty and pain so long as the economy is constantly running at the higher level which is inherent in the new adaptation.

What needs to be borne carefully in mind is that it is not necessarily inflationary to have more money being paid out in wages and salaries to employed labour. It is not necessarily inflationary to pay high overtime rates to labour or to increase take-home pay by making taxation concessions on overtime pay and on wages paid to married women, older persons and others deliberately drawn into the economy through fiscal incentives. Nor is it necessarily deflationary to cut down on wages paid, including payment of overtime, and so to create unemployment. More generally, the supply of money does not, in itself, determine whether a given situation is inflationary, deflationary or just right.

The important thing is the relation between the wages paid (including any fiscal concessions) and production, between the supply of money and the supply of goods. If labour is taking home a great deal more money in its pocket, that is not a bad thing—on the contrary, it is an eminently good thing—so long as production has been increased at least as much as the extra money in labour's pocket, so that the value of money, the value of wages, stability within the economy and stability in the economy's external relations all are maintained. If labour is taking home *less* money in its pocket, that is not a good thing—on the contrary, it is an eminently bad thing—so long as production has been reduced more than demand, so that the value of money and the value of wages are slipping even more than before, instability is still greater in the domestic economy and instability is greater too in the economy's external relations. We must keep in mind therefore that it is not a single economic indicator which usually has most value but the relationship between two or more indicators. In particular, it is not production alone or demand or the supply of money alone which causes inflation or deflation or makes things just right, but the relation between production and demand and the supply of money. We should ask how much is chasing how much and try to keep them equal if we want stability.

What then happens when we set in motion the process for enhancement of production which we have described?

Production is increased. Capital stays at home—and perhaps flows in from abroad. Productivity is, in some respects, enhanced. The gold-rush effect carries the economy to more intensive dynamism, as though there had been a sudden major influx of immigrant labour. In countries like the United States which maintain massive defence forces both at home and overseas, this gold-rush effect, with its gains to production, productivity, monetary stability, equilibrium in the balance of payments and aid and capital flows to developing countries, could be realised by a large-scale reduction in the defence forces, accompanied by expansionist policies aimed at increasing production. It could also be realised by more intensive use of minority-group, especially negro, labour within the community. Although their position has been improving, the blacks in the United States still represent an economically depressed minority and their complete absorption, at a full-employment level, into the national economy could have effects similar in some important ways to the migration of southern labour in Italy to the industrial north.

Finally, we come to the third of those benefits which will accrue from the new adaptation of moving up production to achieve stability at the upper level of the economy. In some ways, this benefit will be the most important of all. Certainly, the benefit will accrue to many more people. This third benefit is the improvement which can be effected in the relations between the developing and the developed countries through the greater resources which will be available—and which will be more *reliably available*—for international aid and development. Here is perhaps the finest contribution which the new adaptation could make to peaceful change in a progressive and harmonious world.

There are other equilibria than those which are strictly economic. Some equilibria are political and some are strategic. Most of them can be assisted and sometimes are completely dependent upon an accompanying economic equilibrium. General de Gaulle said in his 'Mémoires' that 'efficiency and ambition in politics are intertwined with the strength and potential of the economy'. This is a truism which is not always recognised in practice or given the weight it deserves. Political and strategic decisions by governments are too often regarded as simple acts of will, rather than as acts which, in the end, must reflect both will and economic realities. If what people regard as political and strategic imperatives are to be realised, then the economic realities must be in harmony with these imperatives or action must be taken to produce a harmony. Otherwise, political and strategic policies become as fanciful as fairies, as misty as the dreamtime.

The achievement of equilibrium through increased production at the upper level of employment of the economy is the only means of maintaining a high and stable flow of aid and private capital to the developing countries. Without it, the flow in future could become less rather than more—and certainly could be a lesser proportion of gross national product. This is despite the prospective massive increases in the gross national product of most, if not all, of the developed countries. Even if the flow increases—as contemplated in the goals of the Second Development Decade—the increase is likely to be relatively small within the limits imposed by present economic policies. Expansion of production to achieve upper-level equilibrium will not only enlarge the flow but also increase the chances that there will be a regular and reliable increase in international economic and technical aid.

The results can be even greater and more significant than that. They can also allow some countries to continue to play a world role. Not only can they keep the fragile world of the developing countries more stable through economic development but they can also mean that defence aid and support will be more readily available from a number of sources. There is a present threat that those Western countries which have, in the past, helped to maintain political stability and a strategic balance throughout the world may have to withdraw from, or greatly reduce, their world role. That could mean that other countries, with less liberal economic systems, could move into those areas from which the developed Western countries have, either partially or wholly, withdrawn—and could move in, not to play the same role, but to dominate and exploit. Some might dominate on a world scale, others more intensively on a regional scale. Either could be immediately dangerous; both could be ultimately disastrous.

The new theory of general equilibrium could provide a margin against that danger and could contribute vitally to the maintenance of an acceptably benign political and strategic balance. That is not its only, but it could, in the end, constitute its greatest, virtue.

Index